MEDICATION AND FLYING: A PILOT'S GUIDE

by DR. STANLEY R. MOHLER

Boston Publishing Company/Boston, MA

The author and editors wish to acknowledge the contribution made to this book by Aaron M. White, R.Ph., who provided a great deal of the basic research used in developing the individual drug descriptions in chapters 5–10. He offered valuable suggestions and criticism for other parts of the book as well.

Mr. White has considerable experience in this field, having held editorial positions at Houghton Mifflin, PSG Publishing (now John Wright Publishing), and Addison-Wesley. In addition, he has been a technical writer and an assistant professor of biology and genetics. His assistance on this project is much appreciated.

Library of Congress Catalog Card Number: 82–73077

ISBN: 0–939526–04–2

Table of Contents

TABLE OF CONTENTS

Foreword

During the last thirty years the medical profession has witnessed an explosive growth of new pharmaceutical preparations, many with unprecedented power and complexity of effects. Initially both the health care professions and the general public were slow to accept the importance of wide dissemination of appropriate information regarding the actions and proper uses of medicinal drugs. Over the past ten to fifteen years, however, we have witnessed a substantial increase in the interest and effort of many groups to "catch up" with the real information needs of both drug prescribers and consumers.

Many medications and drugs in common use today can impair both mental and physical performance in ways that constitute unacceptable hazards. It is recommended that all flight personnel have access to and an understanding of basic information about the possible influence of medications and drugs on their performance as pilots or ancillary crew.

Flight personnel in civil aviation—be it air carrier, general aviation, air taxi, or commuter—do not usually have available to them the close medical guidance and supervision provided to those in military aviation. Yet the prudent use of medications and drugs is as critical for civilian pilots as for their military counterparts.

Dr. Mohler is to be commended for his circumspective grasp of a complex subject and for his skill in condensing the pertinent information into a format that is logical, lucid, and workable. With proper dissemination, this book will prove to be a most substantial contribution to the judicious use of medications and drugs by flight personnel in all settings.

James W. Long, M.D.

Introduction

It is hoped that this guide will fill a serious information need that has existed for many years in civil aviation. No single guide can be 100 percent applicable to all people, however, and this guide must be used with the appropriate judgment and care. The following information will help the reader use the guide most effectively.

Ideally, a pilot will take no medication whatsoever when flying. Sometimes, however, a pilot can get effective relief from a medical problem by taking a specific type of medicine. This guide provides judgments made by the author and his consultants in aviation medicine and pharmacology concerning pilots' use of specific drugs.

As a practical rule, a pilot should consult an Aviation Medical Examiner (AME) before flying while using any drug. Readers should contact the Federal Aviation Administration (FAA) to learn the names of AMEs practicing in their geographic areas. An FAA Regional Flight Surgeon may also be consulted, as can the FAA Civil Aeromedical Institute in Oklahoma City. A letter to the author will also receive attention; this may be useful if a drug in question is not listed in this guide or if additional information is desired about a particular drug.

From time to time a new drug is discovered. Such a drug may be made available to the public on a limited basis through selected physicians for study until it is fully understood. Pilots who are taking a new medication still under study should fly only after getting clearance from the FAA.

In addition, an approved drug may lose its approval due to the discovery of previously unappreciated adverse effects or of questionable efficacy. This, however, is a fairly rare occurrence.

Specialized medical and pharmaceutical terms are defined as they occur in the text, to help the reader understand more fully the nature and effects of the drugs discussed here.

Specific drugs in this guide are listed alphabetically by generic name within six categories (chapters 5–10) broken down as follows:

I. Flight duties are normally permissible when taking the drug.

INTRODUCTION

II. Flight duties are permissible if approval is given by a flight surgeon (AME or FAA).

III. Flight duties may be approved by the FAA in individual cases.

IV. Flight duties are not permissible until the drug has been discontinued and cleared from the body. Consult a flight surgeon. Check also the individual drug listings in this guide for information on half-life and time needed for significant clearance.

V. The condition being treated precludes flight duties.

VI. The adverse effect of the drug itself precludes flight duties. Check the individual drug listings in this guide for information on half-life and time needed for significant clearance.

Illicit and disapproved drugs are discussed in chapter 4.

There may be disagreement among various physicians on how exactly to categorize specific drugs; additionally, current research and accident studies may bring out new facts that lead to changes in established thinking in this area. The author takes full responsibility for the categorization of drugs listed in this guide and for the information provided about these drugs. All such information is based on the best available knowledge at the time of publication.

Drugs can be located in the index in the back of the book by both their generic and trade names. Various diseases and conditions discussed here are also included in the index.

Some common prefixes and suffixes used in drug names are sometimes omitted here because the root word is usually sufficient for drug identification; for example, the prefixes *oxy, dextro, levo,* and *hydro,* and the suffixes *phosphate, sulfate,* and *hydrochloride.* Exceptions will be found, especially where the prefix or suffix is very commonly used in the name of specific drugs.

Occasionally a state will certify a drug that the federal government does not sanction. For example, Gerovital (procaine HCl), also referred to as "vitamin H_3," has received special approval by the state of Nevada. The substance is also known as Novocain, a local anesthetic. It is felt by some physicians (mostly outside the U.S.) that the substance has rejuvenating effects, but the Food and Drug Administration (FDA) has not determined that the substance has more than a placebo effect when used for this purpose. Accordingly, we do not list the drug here. If it were listed, we would probably place it in category I, as the substance is extremely mild.

Another substance, laetrile, derived from peach pits, has similarly received sanction by certain states but not by the Food and Drug Administration. Because this drug is used for cancer therapy, not infrequently for advanced cases, we would place it in category V. Krebiozen, derived from horse serum, is another unapproved substance alleged to be useful in treating cancer, and it would also be categorized under V.

Since the 1920s, salts of gold have been used for treating certain rheumatoid arthritis victims. These gold compounds come under category V because of the seriousness of the treated condition. Another chemical, DMSO (dimethylsulfoxide), long used in the paper processing industry, is believed by some to relieve rheumatic joint symptoms and accomplish symptomatic relief from other physical problems. Florida and Oregon have approved DMSO for certain purposes, but the FDA has not. DMSO would probably be placed in category II if sanctioned, with a note that it might have adverse effects on the eyes in some people.

Chapter 1

About Drugs: Background and Effects

A drug may be defined as any substance taken beyond the daily nutritional requirements of solid food, water, milk, and fruit juices, with the objective of bringing about a specific result. Alcohol, nicotine, and caffeine are the drugs most frequently taken by self-medication, and all three can have deleterious effects if used to excess.

Supplemental vitamins are not considered drugs unless taken in amounts exceeding several times the daily recommended dose. Nicotine, although addictive, is excepted by the FAA in FAR 67 as a drug of dependence in spite of its many harmful health effects. The use of caffeine, a substance having a much less harmful effect than nicotine, is also excepted by the FAA in FAR 67.

The FAA does not permit medical certification of people addicted to alcohol or other drugs. FAR 91.11 provides for an eight-hour abstinence period from alcohol prior to flight. FAR 91.11 also provides that a pilot must not fly while under the influence of alcohol or any other drug. The word "influence" may be understood as behavioral or physiological effects that adversely modify an individual's judgment, performance, or well-being.

Prescription and Nonprescription Drugs

Certain potentially potent or harmful drugs are required by law to be made available only by prescription from an authorized health practitioner. Others, due to a long history of relatively safe use by self-medication, are available "over the counter" to virtually any buyer. Many of these latter drugs may be relatively ineffective, but if the user believes the drug will work, relief is often achieved.

Medication and Flying concentrates on prescription drugs containing very potent substances. Over-the-counter (OC) drugs containing ingredients that, if available in higher amount, would warrant prescription status are also included in this guide. For example, appetite suppressants containing phenylpropanolamine, a potent substance that can produce hypertension and cardiac failure, are available without prescription. Pilots should not use these OC drugs.

The Controlled Substances Act of 1970 lists five "schedules" of substances that include some of the drugs most dangerous to pilots. A brief summary of these schedules is given in appendix I.

Generic Name and Trade Name

When a drug is developed, it is given a "generic" name, the term that it will be known as regardless of its subsequent "trade" name (or names). This name is officially designated as the United States Adopted Name (USAN) by a special council sponsored by the American Medical Association and the pharmaceutical industry. The term "nonproprietary" is also used for the USAN.

A trade name, or brand name as used here, is assigned by a manufacturer to identify its respective form of a drug preparation. These names are generally registered trademarks, proprietary names that may not be used by any other manufacturer.

Sources of Drugs

A drug may be derived from natural products (for example, oxytetracycline, trademarked Terramycin), or may be entirely a product of laboratory synthesis (for example, the tranquilizer diazepam, trademarked Valium). Some drugs are discovered in nature and later synthesized and routinely produced in the laboratory. The source of a drug has no bearing upon its potency if its purity is held constant and preservatives or other additives do not interact adversely with the original drug.

Some Pharmacologic Terms

A drug is certified as effective and safe by the Food and Drug Administration. (Caution: The "grandfather" approach exempts certain long-used drugs from the effectiveness test.) The drug will have a generic name—a name that may be derived from the chemical formula of the drug (e.g., calcium carbonate, a substance used in some antacids), the source or origin of the drug (e.g., penicillin, originating from the mold, Penicillium notatum), the action of the drug (e.g., nystatin, a substance that inhibits fungus growth), or the historical term describing an effect of the drug (e.g., belladonna—"beautiful lady"—based on its action to dilate the pupils). Other name origins exist, including the total fabrication of a generic name for the beauty of the name (e.g., nylidrin), although this approach is much more common with drug trade names. An approved drug may have more than a dozen trade names and be manufactured by several different companies.

There are more than eight hundred generically named drugs in use. The trade names for these drugs exceed twenty-five hundred. A pilot may ask his physician or pharmacist for the generic name of a medication and use this term when checking on a given drug in this book. The cross-referenced trade names may also be used, but due to the large number of trade names, some may not be included.

Half-Life

The time required to eliminate a drug from the body depends on how much of the drug is in the blood or tissue fluids, but the relative rate at which the drug is eliminated (as a percentage of the amount present) remains constant. The half-life of a drug is defined as the time required to eliminate one-half of the drug present in the body. In general, four times the half-life will see 94 percent of the drug removed.

The removal of all of a drug from the body can take a long time, weeks or longer with some drugs (e.g., bromide, quinine, or arsenic). When the amount remaining in the body falls to very low levels, however, the effect of the drug becomes negligible or of no consequence.

For category IV drugs (chapter 8), multiply the half-life for the drug in question by three to determine the estimated time needed prior to undertaking flight after ceasing drug use. For category VI drugs (chapter 10), many of which are extremely potent, multiply the half-life by five to estimate time needed for effective clearance. Where the half-life is highly variable, assume twenty-four hours as a presumptive half-life.

Data on half-life times may change for some drugs as more research is completed. Also, there will be some variation in half-life depending upon the biological status of an individual, the time of day, and other drugs in the body.

Certain Aspects of Drug Use and Action

Within a range of dose for a specific drug, more of the drug will cause greater effects. Although a drug is usually taken for a specific effect, most drugs have multiple effects. The possibility that one or more of

3

these may be harmful to safe pilot duties must be kept in mind. In addition, two or more drugs taken at the same time may either neutralize or amplify the effects of one another ("synergism"). Alcohol may markedly amplify the nervous system actions of some drugs.

Most drugs are taken by mouth although some are injected, rubbed on the skin, or taken by the inhalation or suppository routes. Some drugs are bound in the stomach or intestines by certain foods and never get effectively into the circulatory system. Absorption of others is delayed by the presence of certain foods. Some drugs are usually taken only with food. Guidance by the physician prescribing the drug or by the drug labeling is mandatory for proper and effective drug use.

Many drugs are made inactive by chemical alteration in the liver and subsequent excretion in the urine. Some are simply excreted directly in the urine. Others may be excreted by the intestinal tract, exhaled by the lungs, lost in sweat, or stored in the hair (where they are subsequently lost as the hair is lost). Some may be stored in fat and slowly let out over a period of time.

As described earlier, there is in general a period of time when half of an internally taken drug is inactivated or eliminated (the half-life). An equal time later, half of the remaining drug is lost, and so on, until the remainder is pharmacologically insignificant.

Unusual Drug Reactions

Drugs may affect an individual differently on different days or at different times of the sleep-wake cycle. In addition, allergies to drugs may develop (especially to penicillin), and idiosyncratic responses may occur with individuals having reactions out of normal proportion to the administered dose.

Some drugs taken continuously over a period of time produce a physical tolerance characterized by the need for increasing amounts of the drug to achieve the desired effect. Psychological dependence or chemical addiction to certain drugs may also occur, an obviously undesirable effect.

Examples of Adverse Drug Effects on Pilots

Drugs can have an enhanced impairing action on the pilot in the presence of fatigue, hypoxia (decreased level of oxygen in the blood), illness, or other drugs. The case histories below illustrate the importance of taking all such factors into account when flying.

Appetite-Suppressing Drugs

A pilot taking dextroamphetamine to suppress his appetite received an adverse weather briefing in a flight service station. Even though a squall line lay across the planned flight route, the pilot's euphoric state eliminated ordinary caution and reason. The briefer commented that the pilot's behavior during the briefing was contrary to that exhibited by other pilots, who tied down their aircraft until the squall line passed. The pilot and his two passengers took off on a visual flight plan toward the squall line and crashed into a mountain during heavy turbulence, killing all on board.

Antihistamines

Periodic problems with an allergy (hay fever) led a pilot to take diphenhydramine (Benadryl) from time to time. On one occasion, while regularly taking this drug, the pilot became so drowsy during a night flight that an unplanned landing became imperative. Unlike automobile driving, there is no "pulling to the side of the road" for sleepy pilots when the effects of a drug become manifest.

Sedatives

A student pilot approaching the point of solo, after about eleven hours of training, suddenly became unable to progress and actually regressed in skill. The instructor and the student were unable to explain this turn of events until a fellow airplane club member, a physician, learned that the student had recently been put on Donnatal—a mixture of barbiturate, atropine, and hyoscine—for a "nervous stomach." After discontinuing the medication no further flight problems occurred.

Nasal Decongestants

A slight nasal and sinus congestion was causing discomfort to a pilot. He took an ephedrine decongestant and, receiving relief, proceeded on a cross-country flight. During the flight, however, the decongestant wore off. Upon descending from cruise altitude, the pilot experienced excruciating sinus and middle ear pain. He had to climb somewhat to relieve the pain and work his way down, never fully without symptoms during the approach and for several hours after landing. The transitory nature of drug effects is a key factor for consideration, which is one reason why the information here on half-lives is so valuable.

5

MEDICATION AND FLYING: A PILOT'S GUIDE

Pain Medication

A pilot flying cross-country with his family on board was taking pain medicine to relieve the renal colic caused by a troublesome kidney stone. The pain medicine's effect wore off, and the pilot attempted a landing in the countryside because he could not continue flying with the incapacitating pain. The aircraft struck a house, killing the pilot and passengers.

Tranquilizers

A pilot began to experience some anxieties and went to a psychiatrist who prescribed a common tranquilizer. One day, while tranquilized, the usually competent airline pilot continued flying past a fix where a turn was required. The continued flight took the aircraft into a mountain, with fatal consequences to all but one of the occupants.

Ganglionic Blocking Agent

A pilot was surreptitiously taking a potent antihypertensive drug, one that can produce too low a blood pressure, with dizziness to loss of consciousness possible on sudden standing. While accelerating in a pitch-up maneuver the pilot apparently blacked out. The plane rolled over and dived straight into the ground.

Chapter 2

The Most Widely Used Drug: Alcohol

Alcohol is a drug by any definition and all pilots should be aware of its properties. A pilot cannot safely mix flying with alcohol, including its hangover effects.

People "medicate" themselves with alcohol to change their state of consciousness. This change is a chemically induced tendency toward euphoria, resulting in a reduction in anxiety. Alcohol may also be taken as a form of medication by people seeking temporary relief from their depression.

People addicted to alcohol require it daily in order to prevent withdrawal symptoms. Professional treatment is necessary for withdrawal and abstinence.

Ethyl alcohol is an addictive drug and it would no doubt immediately be placed under the jurisdiction of the Food and Drug Administration if it were first discovered today. Chemical analyses of alcoholic beverages, including their levels of purity, would no doubt be provided to alcohol users, as is done with other drugs. Alcohol consumption per adult in the United States averages twenty-five gallons per year, indicating the exposure of many persons to psychoactive beverages that are neither controlled by the Food and Drug Administration nor monitored by it. This is the only federal agency with the scientific expertise to accomplish these functions.

Categories of Alcoholic Beverages

Alcoholic beverages may be classified in three major categories (see table 2-1). In general, the lower the concentration of alcohol in a given beverage, the greater the quantity of volume in a single serving (e.g., the shot glass of whiskey versus the tumbler of beer). A given "standard" drink in one category thus may be defined as approximately equal in alcohol to a "standard" drink in any other category. In other words, three shots of whiskey equal three bottles of beer in alcohol content.

TABLE 2-1   Types of Alcoholic Beverages

I. Fermented but not distilled
   A. Grapes (natural, sparkling, fortified wines)
   B. Fruits (cider, perry)
   C. Grain (beer, ale, stout, porter, sake)
   D. Miscellaneous (pulque)
II. Distilled
   A. Grain (whiskey, vodka)
   B. Sugar cane molasses (rum)
   C. Agave (tequila)
   D. Fruits (grape, apple, cherry, plum brandy)
   E. Ti root (okolehao)
III. Compounded (flavored spirits)
   A. Gin
   B. Akvavit
   C. Liqueur
   D. Absinthe
   E. Bitters

Note: The major categories of alcoholic beverages are traditionally broken down as shown above.

Alcohol Consumption and the Human Body

Alcohol is metabolized in the liver, yielding the chemical acetaldehyde. Acetaldehyde has toxic effects on the nervous system. It is a major factor causing the nausea and headache often experienced following excessive alcohol intake.

The metabolism of alcohol to acetaldehyde by the liver, in addition to other alcoholic effects, produces brain edema, or swelling. A pounding headache may accompany this reaction (thought to be the result of dilated cranial veins). Irritability, agitation, and depression are additional responses. Continuous cycling through these states, often leading to an increasing intake of alcohol, impairs pilot competency. Alcohol may also interact with other drugs, often resulting in magnified effects detrimental to the individual.

Many alcoholic beverages are not fit for human consumption because they contain large amounts of various additives, congeners (fusel oils), and other toxic substances. This is especially true of "moonshine" liquor and many cheap whiskeys and wines. The Food and Drug Administration does not check for the safety of additives in alcoholic beverages.

Several years ago a number of people in the United States died because of such an additive: cobalt. Cobalt compounds were added to certain beers by brewers so that more foam would form when the beer was poured. As a result of cobalt poisoning, some beer drinkers' hearts became dilated and weak, causing heart failure.

To help assure that an alcoholic beverage is "safe," request the more expensive name brands produced by reputable houses. (A side benefit of this is that people tend to drink less if it costs more.) Some producers mix bad products with good products, resulting in a product that may contain large amounts of congeners, substances implicated in contributing to hangovers. Labels may someday specify exactly what is contained in the bottles, including the additives. The beverage's aging history should also be specified where appropriate.

Alcohol moves rapidly from the stomach to the blood, which carries it to all parts of the body. It reaches the brain within fifteen seconds and the amount of alcohol in the brain stabilizes to match that in the blood. The brain undergoes an "acute toxic brain syndrome," resulting in an illusion of emotional and physical well-being. Fatigue sensations begin to abate as do slight physical discomforts. Often, muscle and joint soreness begin to disappear as alcohol is consumed. Increasing sensations of strength, well-being, and capability, including courage, occur. Performance derogation in skilled athletic events occurs. This derogation affects other types of performance as well, including pilot performance. The greater the amount of alcohol consumed, the greater the impairment of performance. And the impairment sometimes lingers; hangover effects have been shown to cause a sevenfold increase of errors in preflight planning.

Should an individual use ethyl alcohol regularly, three identifiable personalities will appear in repeated sequence:

1. Normal sobriety—personality A
2. Inebriated euphoria—personality A'
3. The agitation and depression of withdrawal—personality A"

Individuals experiencing personality states A' and A" are hazards in the air as well as on the ground.

Blood Alcohol Level

Blood alcohol decreases at about .015 percent per hour. Table 2-2 gives estimated percentages of alcohol in the blood for various body weights. A blood alcohol level of .040 percent has been shown to seriously impair pilot performance. One average drink (.015 percent blood alcohol) will produce enough change in mental function to derogate pilot performance.

TABLE 2-2 Blood Alcohol Level (%)

Body Weight in Pounds	Number of Drinks (Average)											
	1	2	3	4	5	6	7	8	9	10	11	12
100	.038	.075	.113	.150	.188	.225	.263	.300	.338	.375	.413	.450
120	.031	.063	.094	.125	.156	.188	.219	.250	.281	.313	.344	.375
140	.027	.054	.080	.107	.134	.161	.188	.214	.241	.268	.295	.321
160	.023	.047	.070	.094	.117	.141	.164	.188	.211	.234	.258	.281
180	.021	.042	.063	.083	.104	.125	.146	.167	.188	.208	.229	.250
200	.019	.038	.056	.075	.094	.113	.131	.150	.169	.188	.206	.225
220	.017	.034	.051	.068	.085	.102	.119	.136	.153	.170	.188	.205
240	.016	.031	.047	.063	.078	.094	.109	.125	.141	.156	.172	.188

Note: .015 percent blood alcohol is equal to "15 mg percent," .100 percent blood alcohol equals "100 mg percent," etc.

The concentration of blood alcohol reaches a higher level and is maintained longer at higher altitudes. This was confirmed in 1936 in tests conducted by Dr. R. A. McFarland. An airman who ascends to even moderate altitudes with alcohol in the blood would be especially vulnerable to the alcohol effects. For example, the alcohol in two or three cocktails would have the physiological action of four or five drinks or more at altitudes of ten to twelve thousand feet. See figure 2–1 below.

FIGURE 2-1

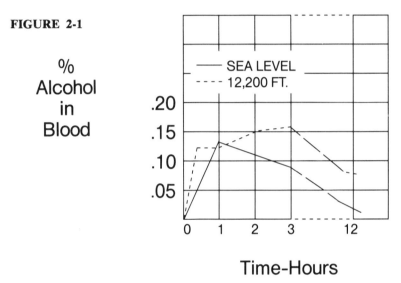

%
**Alcohol
in
Blood**

Time-Hours

Source: McFarland, R. A., and Forbes, W. H. "The Metabolism of Alcohol in Man at High Altitudes." *Human Biology.* 8 (1936): 387–398.

Behavior changes are similar whether due to oxygen lack or the influence of alcohol. Complex mental functions, the ability to concentrate, and feelings of euphoria accompany both hypoxia and alcohol intake. The effects of both are insidious in onset and adversely affect judgment. Alone, each is hazardous; together, the hazards are magnified.

Alcohol Intake and Flying

Ideally, a pilot will be the same individual whether at home, at work, or flying an airplane. (In some cases, flying an airplane may be the "work.") If alcohol is consumed, it should be at minimal levels, so as not to change significantly the personality or other mental capacities.

11

This means that one or two ounces of alcohol, no more than once or twice a week, should be the upper intake guideline for most people.

As early as World War I, flight surgeons warned that alcohol "excitement," or drunkenness, was a cause of foolish flight decisions by pilots. As recently as January 13, 1977, a DC-8 airline aircraft bound for Japan over-rotated on takeoff and crashed at Anchorage, Alaska. The three members of the crew died in the crash as did the entire cargo of cattle. The National Transportation Safety Board (NTSB) reported that the captain's impairment by alcohol caused the accident. The postaccident studies showed that the captain had a blood alcohol level of .210 percent (equivalent to ten drinks for a 180-pound person).

Alcohol has been an associated factor in fatal general aviation accidents, decreasing from 43 percent in 1963 to about 16 percent at present. Pilot safety programs' emphasis on the hazards of mixing alcohol with flying and the eight-hour abstinence rule (FAR 91.11) have both contributed to this decrease, but the number of alcohol-associated accidents is still much too high. Objective inflight studies have shown that .040 percent blood alcohol (three alcoholic drinks) is exceedingly detrimental to flight performance.

Daily consumption of alcohol, even as little as an ounce per day, causes the development of an increased tolerance. With increasing tolerance, more alcohol must be consumed to exceed the new tolerance level and produce the desired euphoric response. Under these conditions, the nervous system undergoes acute withdrawal when alcohol is metabolized, resulting in a transitory agitated state. Alcohol causes retention of sodium by the kidneys, and this increase in body sodium level produces tissue excitability. This is aggravated by a concomitant loss of magnesium, a nervous system inhibitor of excitability.

Alcohol and Body Organs

Alcohol has adverse effects on every organ in the body. These adverse effects will be found in persons who drink several ounces of alcohol or more per day. The following sections list alcohol's adverse effects.

Brain and Other Central Nervous System Components

- impaired abstract reasoning and judgment (cognition)
- impaired memory
- impaired creativity
- impaired coordination by cerebellum
- distortion of reality
- changes of mood

- depression
- development of self-destructive behavior
- insomnia or soporific effect

Peripheral Nervous System

- delayed and lengthened reaction time

Muscles

- inflamed muscles (myositis)
- decreased muscle tone

Skeleton

- anesthetized joints with hyper-extension injury
- depressed bone marrow with decrease in all blood cell types

Cardiovascular System

- cardiac muscle myositis
- enlarged heart (15–25 percent, acute effect of alcohol)

Kidneys

- excessive sodium retention
- excessive magnesium loss

Liver

- shutoff of glucose production from protein
- excessive activation of fat pathways with "fatty liver" development

Pancreas

- damage to cellular structure, with internal digestive enzyme liberation and pancreatitis

- cerebral atrophy (Korsakoff's syndrome, Wernicke's syndrome)
- headache

- neuritis

- muscle "pulls" and injuries

- synovial (pertaining to joint membranes) and tendon sheath fluid change, with joint and tendon damage during physical stresses (arthritic changes)

- hypertension
- sludging of red blood cells

- excessive water retention after several ounces of alcohol

- inability to fully produce testosterone, with estrogen buildup in males

13

Endocrine System

- excessively high or low insulin
- breast development in males

Gastrointestinal System

- hyperirritability alternating with hypofunction (diarrhea followed by flatulence and constipation)
- indigestion, nausea, vomiting
- inflammation of the esophagus (esophagitis) and erosive gastritis; gum degeneration
- impairment of absorption of vitamins

Skin

- flushing (reddening) due to small vessel dilation
- destruction of sebaceous cell tissue of nose giving larger, reddish nose

Genitalia, Including Reproductive Organs

- impairment of erection in males
- direct damage to developing embryo, including brain impairment and other abnormalities during development

Sensory Organs

- eye muscle imbalance, tending toward double vision when fusion is broken
- inner ear hydrops (edema) with relative deafness and dizziness on motion
- twenty-four hours later, positional alcohol nystagmus (oscillation of the eyes when head is moved)

Blood Tests

- elevated uric acid, serum triglycerides, and various enzymes, including especially serum gamma glutamyl transpetidase, which will be elevated the day following consumption of two alcoholic drinks

Pulmonary System

- emphysema due to coagulation of alveolar wall cells by alcohol fumes
- paralysis of cilia (tiny moving hairs in the bronchial tree that sweep foreign particles up and out of the lungs)
- vocal cord thickening, resulting in "gravel" voice

14

Increased Rates of Cancer

- mouth, larynx, esophagus,
  lung, and liver cancer

Increased Proneness to Accidents and to Death

- 2.5 times higher death rate than nonalcoholic controls
- medical costs estimated at $24 billion due to alcohol-related illnesses and injuries, with two-thirds of hospitalizations related to alcohol
- stressed intoxicated heart muscle may suddenly fail on extreme muscular exertion

Bibliography

Billings, C. E., Wick, R. L., Gerke, R. J., and Chase, R. C. "The Effects of Alcohol on Pilot Performance During Instrument Flight." *Office of Aviation Medicine Report No. FA-AM-72-4.* Washington, D.C.: Federal Aviation Administration, 1972.

Collins, W. E. "Performance Effects of Alcohol Intoxication and Hangover at Ground Level and at Simulated Altitude." *Office of Aviation Medicine Report No. FA-AM-79-26.* Washington, D.C.: Federal Aviation Administration, 1979.

Collins, W. E., and Chiles, W. D. "Laboratory Performance During Acute Intoxication and Hangover." *Office of Aviation Medicine Report No. FA-AM-79-7.* Washington, D.C.: Federal Aviation Administration, 1979.

Gould, L. "Whiskey and Cardiac Function." *Chest.* 63 (1973): 943–947.

Grossman, H. J. *Grossman's Guide to Wines, Spirits, and Beers.* New York: Charles Scribner's Sons, 1964.

Harper, C. R., and Albers, W. R. "Alcohol and General Aviation Accidents." *Aerospace Medicine.* 35 (1964): 462.

Harper, E. O. "Alcohol." Vol. 6, No. 19, Psychiatry Series. Glendale, California: Audio-Digest Foundation, 1977.

Jacobson, M., and Anderson, J. "The Chemical Additives in Booze." Center for Science in The Public Interest, September 1972.

Jordanoff, A. *Safety In Flight.* New York: Funk and Wagnalls Co., 1941, pp. 127–128.

Mohler, S. R. "Pilots and Alcohol: Mix with Caution." *Human Factors Bulletin.* Flight Safety Foundation, September/December 1980.

Mohler, S. R. "Recent Findings on the Impairment of Airmanship by Alcohol." *Office of Aviation Medicine Report No. AM-66-29.* Washington, D.C.: Federal Aviation Administration, September 1966.

National Transportation Safety Board. "Aircraft Accident Report, Japan Airlines Co. Ltd. McDonnell Douglas DC-8-62F, JA 8054, Anchorage, Alaska, Jan. 13, 1977." NTSB Report No. AAR-78-7. Washington, D.C.: National Transportation Safety Board, January 16, 1979, pp. 1–77.

Nunez, B. E. "Wine: In Sickness and in Health." *The Vinifera Wine Growers Journal.* 1 (Spring 1974).

Parker, E. S., and Noble, E. P. "Alcohol Consumption and Cognitive Functioning in Social Drinkers." *Journal of Studies on Alcohol.* 38 (1974): 1224–1232.

Paton, A., and Saunders, J. B. "ABC of Alcohol." *British Medical Journal.* 283 (November 7, 1981): 14.

Public Law 91-616. The Comprehensive Alcohol Abuse and Alcoholism Prevention, Treatment and Rehabilitation Act, 1970.

Rand Corporation. "Four Year Study of Alcohol Abuse and Longevity." Rockville, Maryland: National Institute on Alcohol Abuse and Alcoholism, 1980.

Ryan, L. C., and Mohler, S. R. "The Current Role of Alcohol as a Factor in Civil Aviation Aircraft Accidents." *Office of Aviation Medicine Report No. FAA-AM-80-4.* Washington, D.C.: Federal Aviation Administration, May 1–10, 1980.

Ryan, L. C., and Mohler, S. R. "Intoxicating Liquor and the General Aviation Pilot in 1971." *Aerospace Medicine.* 43 (1972): 1024–1026.

Ryback, R. S., and Dowd, P. J. "After Effects of Various Alcoholic Beverages on Positional Nystagmus and Coriolis Acceleration." *Aerospace Medicine.* 41 (1970): 429–435.

War Department. *Air Service Medical.* Washington, D.C.: U.S. Government Printing Office, 1919, p. 130.

Wharton, L. "Sedativism." *Educational Brochure.* Oklahoma City, Oklahoma: Aeromedical Education Branch, Federal Aviation Administration, 1980.

Wise, L. M. "Residual Effect of Alcohol on Aircrew Performance." *SAFE Journal.* 10 (1980): 28–31.

Wolkenberg, R. C., Gold, C., and Tichauer, E. R. "Delayed Effects of Acute Alcoholic Intoxication on Performance with Reference to Work Safety." *Journal of Safety Research.* 7 (1975): 104–118.

Chapter 3

Nicotine and the Pilot

A pilot who enjoys flying and hopes to avoid grounding due to heart disease, emphysema, malignancy, or other illnesses related to tobacco use should not be a smoker. On July 28, 1979, the surgeon general of the United States reported that cigarette smoking is the single most preventable cause of death today. Many smokers will have years of breathing disability and heart disease in midlife and later. Smokers may also develop a lifestyle that essentially focuses on their next cigarette. For the smoking pilot this adds an additional workload before, during, and after flight. For those around the pilot during flight, the tobacco smoke and odors can be irritating and even nauseating.

Smoking, chewing, and sniffing tobacco are all methods of introducing nicotine, a toxic drug, into the body. Nicotine is potentially addictive, as are alcohol, opium, morphine, codeine, heroin, meperidine, or barbiturates.

The nicotine user experiences a chemically modified mood, the sensation of lessened fatigue. Some may feel a degree of euphoria. Within twenty to thirty minutes, withdrawal begins moving individuals back toward ordinary feelings. This is accompanied, however, by an awareness that the thought process is slowing down. Fatigue sensations also develop. These withdrawal symptoms are harder to bear under mental or physical stress. For regular smokers, the discomfort increases after several hours; irritability appears, accompanied by developing aggression and feelings of hostility. As increasing tolerance is a characteristic of addiction, smokers will often increase their frequency of smoking.

Nicotine is a tobacco plant "alkaloid." When pure, it has little odor. It gradually decomposes, producing the characteristic tobacco aroma. Nicotine assumes a dark brown color as it decomposes.

Physiologically, nicotine acts on the central nervous system (brain and spinal cord), skeletal muscle nerve endings or voluntary nervous system, and the "ganglia" of the automatic or involuntary nervous system. All of these actions produce complex toxic physiological effects that are not always immediately apparent.

In the United States, 54 million of the 230 million population, a little more than 23 percent, are smokers. In 1950 the average cigarette had about 36 mg of "tar," while in 1979 the figure was about 17 mg. The 1950 nicotine amount per cigarette was about 2 mg, dropping to about 1.1 mg today. Cigarettes are available today with less than 10 mg of tar and less than 1 mg of nicotine. As a rule, the lower the tar and nicotine, the longer the period before lung cancer, heart disease, bronchitis, or other illnesses are apt to develop. When menthol is added to cigarettes to make them burn "cool," it functions to anesthetize the sensory nerves in the throat, simply simulating "coolness"; this in no way alters the effects of the tar and nicotine in these cigarettes.

About forty-eight hundred chemicals have been isolated from cigarette smoke. Many of these have proven toxic and cancer-causing qualities. Included are nitrosamine, vinyl chloride, polonium-210, formaldehyde, hydrogen cyanide, acrolein, acetaldehyde, nitrogen oxides, benzopyrene, benzoanthracene, fluoranthene, phenol, nicotine, and carbon monoxide.

Regular cigarette smokers develop a blood carbon monoxide level (as carboxyhemoglobin) of about 5 percent, which reduces the blood oxygen level to that of a nonsmoking person at an altitude of about seven thousand feet above sea level. The pilot who is also a smoker will thus tend to become relatively more hypoxic at lower altitudes than will a nonsmoking pilot. The following example and chart illustrate the potential dangers of this enhanced susceptibility to hypoxia.

A military pilot, a nonsmoker, was flying alone in a T-28 out of Pensacola at night in bad weather. While flying IFR at fifteen thousand feet, his oxygen failed in the unpressurized aircraft, and he immediately requested permission to descend to a lower altitude. This permission was slightly delayed because of the weather and heavy air traffic, but the pilot was able finally to bring the aircraft down to an altitude where oxygen would not be a concern and completed the flight without any further problems.

He related to an AME later that he was unaware of the oxygen failure until he felt the symptoms of hypoxia, and by that time it was becoming somewhat difficult for him to control the plane and to communicate clearly with ground control personnel. The AME suggested it was fortunate the pilot was not a smoker; his altitude in that case would effectively have been twenty-two thousand feet, and his time of useful consciousness (TUC) because of hypoxia would have been significantly decreased (see table 3-1). The extra margin of time he had by virtue of being a nonsmoker may well have prevented a more serious, possibly fatal incident.

TABLE 3-1   **Time of Useful Consciousness (TUC) Without Oxygen By Altitude**

ALTITUDE	TUC
40,000 ft.	15 seconds
35,000 ft.	20 seconds
30,000 ft.	30 seconds
28,000 ft.	1 minute
26,000 ft.	2 minutes
24,000 ft.	3 minutes
22,000 ft.	6 minutes
20,000 ft.	10 minutes
15,000 ft.	Indefinite

Source: Mohler, S. R. "Physiologically Tolerable Decompression Profiles for Supersonic Transport Type Certification." *Office of Aviation Medicine Report AM 70-12*, Washington, D.C.: Federal Aviation Administration, July 1970.

Cigarette Smoking's Life-Shortening Effects

Smoking-related diseases are such important causes of disability and premature death in developed countries that the control of cigarette smoking could do more to improve health and prolong life in these countries than any single action in the whole field of preventive medicine (World Health Organization, Geneva, 1970). Dr. Jesse Steinfeld, former U.S. surgeon general, points out that the two-pack-a-day smoker who is thirty years old will statistically live eight-and-a-half years less than a comparable nonsmoker.

Medically Disqualifying Diseases Caused by Cigarette Smoking

The National Cancer Institute has found that one of every five days smokers miss from work because of illness is due to smoking. One of every ten days smokers spend sick in bed is due to their cigarette addiction. The institute stresses that smoking causes fatigue, headaches, chronic cough, halitosis, nervousness, shortness of breath, and poor general health. The U.S. Public Health Service reports that in 1976 cigarette smoking was responsible for sixty-eight thousand of the eighty-four thousand lung cancer deaths in the United States and one-fourth of the deaths from heart disease. Since heart disease is the leading cause of deaths in the United States, causing half of all deaths, the adverse effects of smoking require serious attention.

19

Scientists have found that coughing and phlegm production due to inhaled irritants is directly related to the number of cigarettes smoked. Nicotine slows or stops the action of the tiny cleansing filaments (cilia) in the respiratory tract, predisposing smokers to tracheitis and bronchitis. Smokers experience respiratory infections more frequently, and smoking is responsible for 70 percent of emphysema and chronic bronchitis cases.

A chronic complaint of smokers is shortness of breath on exertion and a progressive deterioration of physical fitness. In the United States about twenty-five thousand respiratory deaths (primarily from emphysema and related conditions) each year are caused by smoking. In addition, the U.S. Public Health Service reports that cigarette smokers have much higher rates of cancer of the larynx, pharynx, mouth, esophagus, pancreas, and urinary bladder.

Cigarette smoking also affects the cardiac risk factor in women. It has been demonstrated that smoking thirty-five cigarettes or more a day increases by twenty times the rate of heart attack in women. If oral contraceptive drugs are taken, cigarette smoking further increases the risk of heart attack, especially in women older than thirty-five. Postmenopausal women have a significantly higher risk of developing osteoporosis if they are smokers.

Nicotine may cause degeneration of certain parts of the retina (amblyopia) resulting in blind spots in the visual field. All people, smokers and nearby nonsmokers, experience direct irritating effects on the corneal and conjunctival tissues of the eyes from contact with the tobacco combustion products. Acute inflammation of the eyes and squinting accompany smoking. Cabin air is often very dry, especially in pressurized aircraft, causing the irritating effects of tobacco smoke to increase.

Another side effect of smoking is that smokers eliminate caffeine twice as fast as nonsmokers, sometimes leading to greater coffee intake by smokers than nonsmokers. The therapeutic effectiveness of a number of drugs is reduced because of their more rapid elimination in smokers.

Nicotine Withdrawal Problems

When a nicotine-dependent individual is deprived of the substance, mental functions—especially problem solving—seem impaired. The ensuing agitation leads to self-centered thoughts concentrated on finding a cigarette. Hand tremor and insomnia are common symptoms of withdrawal.

Unexpected layovers because of weather or diversions to alternates at late hours in out-of-the-way places may exhaust the pilot's supply of cigarettes. Irritability and the other problems of withdrawal can then become added burdens to affected pilots.

Chronic Insomnia

The nicotine addict requires an "infusion" every forty-five minutes to avoid withdrawal effects. Smokers may wake craving nicotine, have a cigarette, and then go back to sleep. This may occur several times each night. The nicotine-deprived brain thus cannot obtain a restful night's sleep. A chronic state of sleep loss and insomnia through sleep deprivation increases irritability while awake.

Involuntary Smokers

"Sidestream" smoke, arising from the burning core of tobacco, is involuntarily inhaled by people nearby. The smoker's exhaled smoke, referred to as "mainstream" smoke, is similarly inhaled by those nearby. As a result, a smoker converts other cockpit members into passive smokers.

Mainstream smoke contains half of the original carbon monoxide level of sidestream smoke. Added to the sidestream smoke, however, it carries relatively high concentrations of carbon monoxide, nicotine, and other substances to the passive smokers.

Fouled Gyroscopic Instruments and Outflow Valves

Gyroscopic instruments drawing cockpit air can become fouled and outflow valves in pressurized aircraft can become gummed because of tobacco tar. The progressive accumulation of tobacco tar and other chemicals in these sensitive mechanical components may cause instrument malfunction and failure at a much earlier point in an instrument's life than would otherwise occur. The most common cause of pressurization system malfunction (including decompressions) is tobacco tar accumulation in outflow valves. Outflow valves begin to stick in the closed, partially open, or full open positions as the tar collects, markedly escalating maintenance costs as flight operation pressure problems occur. This can also increase malfunction downtime and inflight emergencies resulting from gyroscopic instrument failure. The potential for adverse flight safety effects caused by cigarette smoke is clear.

Kicking the Habit

Some smokers may feel that they are hopelessly hooked on nicotine and that they are doomed to live the remainder of their lives as addicts. The smoker who quits before irreversible pathology develops will have an improved mortality outlook after ten to fifteen years that is almost the same as that of the nonsmoker. This alone is sufficient justification for the pilot-smoker to decide to quit smoking. Programs are available throughout the country that assist those seeking to stop smoking.

Once the acute withdrawal phase (one to two weeks) is past, the new nonsmoker may gain a sense of "unaddicted health." Sleep will occur more readily, be more refreshing, and be of shorter duration, allowing more time for other activities. Quitting does not cause weight gain if caloric intake is not increased.

The National Cancer Institute has a free kit that will give guidance on quitting smoking. The institute will mail it on request to those interested. The address is National Cancer Institute, 9000 Rockville Pike, Bethesda, MD 20205.

The first six months after quitting are the most critical. After that, the body is cleared of the nicotine and related toxic substances and will have returned to a healthier biological state. A former smoker may be vulnerable to returning to smoking during periods of stress. In addition, many exsmokers find that alcohol affects them more when not smoking. Instead of drinking less, some may start smoking again to counter the effects of alcohol. Anticipating these effects will help those who have quit smoking avoid a relapse by adopting countermeasures.

Bibliography

Bronson, Thomas E. "Smoking: A Safety Hazard for Air Force Aircrews." Alabama: Air University, Maxwell Air Force Base, May 1978.

Director General, Civil Aviation. "Prohibition of Smoking During Flight: Civil Aviation Regulations." USSR: Ministry of Civil Aviation, Fall 1977.

Expert Panel. "Cigarette Smoking and Airline Pilots: Effects of Smoking and Smoking Withdrawal on Flight Performance." Bethesda, Maryland: National Institutes of Health, April 1978.

FDA Drug Bulletin. "Clinical Implications of Surgeon General's Report on Smoking and Health." Washington, D.C., February/March 1979.

"Helping Smokers Quit Kit." Department K-88 (no charge), National Cancer Institute, Bethesda, Maryland 20205.

Kannel, W. B., Castelli, W. P., and McNamara, P. M. *Cigarette Smoking and Risk of Coronary Heart Disease—Epidemiologic Clues to Pathogen-*

esis—The Framingham Study. Monograph, National Cancer Institute. 28 (1968): 9–20.

Mohler, S. R. "The Dedicated Pilot: No Nicotine Addict." *Human Factors Bulletin.* Flight Safety Foundation, July/August 1979.

Schecter, M. D., and Rand, M. J. "Effect of Acute Deprivation of Smoking on Aggression and Hostility." *Psychopharmacologia.* 35 (1974): 19–28.

Sloane, D., Shapiro, S., Rosenberg, I., Kaufman, D. W., Hartz, S. C., Rossi, A. C., Stolley, P. D., and Miettinen, O. S. "Relation of Cigarette Smoking to Myocardial Infarction in Young Women." *New England Journal of Medicine.* 23 (June 8, 1978): 1273–1276.

Steinfeld, Jesse L. "Passive Smoker Studies Called Neglected Area." *U.S. Medicine.* 15 (February 15, 1979).

Surgeon General, U.S. Navy. Letter to Navy Doctors. Washington, D.C.: U.S. Navy, September 21, 1977.

U.S. Department of Health, Education and Welfare. *The Health Consequences of Smoking.* Atlanta, Georgia: Center for Disease Control, 1976.

Wynder, E. L., and Hoffman, D. "Tobacco and Health." *New England Journal of Medicine.* (April 19, 1979): 894–903.

Chapter 4

Illicit and Disapproved Drugs

There are certain drugs that society prohibits due to their uniformly harmful effects. A competent pilot should not voluntarily use these drugs. Certain illicit drugs (e.g., LSD and marijuana) can cause "flashbacks"—hallucinatory phenomena occurring days or weeks after taking the drug when some of the drug, previously stored in the body, is released. If this happens in flight, one can imagine the potential adverse effects.

Illicit Drugs

Angel Dust (Phencyclidine)

This is an animal tranquilizer that causes severe mental function aberrance. Memory is extremely impaired and anxiety sensations may be overwhelming. This substance is also known as PCP.

Cocaine (benzomethyl ecognine)

This substance produces extreme mood elevation, elation, and grandiose feelings followed by a deep depression. Repeated use leads to paranoid delusions and antisocial behavior.

Hashish (the resin from the female hemp plant, Cannabis sativa)

The active chemical in hashish is THC: tetrahydrocannabinol. This drug produces debilitation of will. It has a strong tendency to lead to psychic dependence by the user, causing distortions of sensations and delusions of grandeur.

Heroin (diacetylmorphine hydrochloride)

This drug is extremely addictive. It causes a state of euphoria and produces a state of "half-sleep."

LSD (d-lysergic acid diethylamide tartrate)

This dangerous substance causes hallucinations and distortions of perceptions and sensations. Acute psychoses and suicidal tendencies may occur. Flashbacks may occur months after use.

Marijuana (Cannabis sativa)

The leaf of the marijuana plant is the part most often smoked. As in hashish, the active ingredient is tetrahydrocannabinol (THC). The effects are euphoria, sensations of body distortion, and sensations of a slowing of time. Disturbances of memory may occur.

Mescaline (trimethoxyphenylethylamine)

This substance comes from the peyote cactus and causes hallucinations and sensation distortion.

Morning Glory Seeds

These were used by Aztec Indians for the hallucinatory effects produced by a tea made from them. The hallucinations and distorted thinking patterns they cause may lead to highly irrational behavior and even suicide.

STP (4-methyl-2, 5-dimethoxy-a-methyl phenethylamine)

This chemical causes toxic psychoses in spite of its nickname, "serenity, tranquility, and peace."

Disapproved Drugs

The Food and Drug Administration reviews a New Drug Application (NDA) for each new drug. If it is determined that a specific drug is unsafe (designated as WDS: withdrawn on the basis of safety) or ineffective (designated as WDE: withdrawn for lack of efficacy), the drug is not approved for marketing or is withdrawn from the market if previously approved.

The following list gives some examples of drugs falling in the WDS and WDE categories. Any of these drugs that might be lying around medicine cabinets should be discarded.

Withdrawn for Lack of Safety

generic name	trade name	comment
Azaribine	Triazure	WDS 6/10/77 causes blood clots
Medroxyprogesterone with ester diol	Provest	WDS 3/16/72 causes tumors

26

generic name	trade name	comment
Mestranol and chlormadinone	C-Quens	WDS 3/16/72 causes blood clots
Methanesulfonate of aminopyrine	Dipyrone	WDS 6/17/77 causes agranulocytosis
Potassium chloride enteric coated	Potassium chloride enteric	WDS 7/29/77 causes stomach and intestinal ulcers
Ticrynafen	Selacryn	WDS 1980 causes liver damage
Triparanol	MER-29	WDS 1961 causes cataracts

Withdrawn for Lack of Efficacy

generic name	trade name	comment
Anisotropine	Valpin	WDE 7/13/79
Mebutamate hydrochlorothiazide	Caplaril	WDE 10/18/73
Penicillinase	Nutrapen	WDE 9/29/75
Pentaerythrityl tetranitrate with phenobarbital	Peritrate with phenobarbital	WDE 1/25/80

Chapter 5

Category I Drugs: Flight Duties
Are Normally Permissible

Flight duties are normally permissible when taking any of the drugs in this category. Refer to the individual drug listings here for more specific information about a drug's effects on flight activities. As always, consult an AME or the FAA if any question remains about the advisability of flying while taking one of these drugs.

Generic name: *acetaminophen*
Brand names: (many, including *Tylenol*)
Multi-ingredient drugs: (many)
Usual dose: 1.5–2 gm per day

Acetaminophen is an over-the-counter drug used to relieve mild headaches and joint and muscle pains. It may also be used to reduce fever.

Acetaminophen is widely used by people allergic to aspirin as an alternative. Adverse side effects are few, though occasional stomach irritation may occur. Use of acetaminophen does not of itself interfere with flying, although the condition for which it is taken may (e.g., a hangover or a head cold).

The half-life of acetaminophen is about three hours. Nine hours after the last dose, no more than about 12 percent is present in the body.

Generic name: *acetylsalicylic acid*
Synonym: *aspirin*
Brand names: (many)
Multi-ingredient drugs: (many)
Usual dose: .6–2.4 gm per day

Acetylsalicylic acid (aspirin) is the most commonly used of all drugs. It is taken to relieve mild pain or headache and to reduce fever.

Aspirin has few adverse side effects. It can irritate the stomach lining, although many are not bothered by this irritation. Buffered aspirin may cut down on any irritating effects, but some may find it necessary to use a different drug, such as acetaminophen, to avoid stomach irritation. This is especially true of those who are allergic to aspirin.

The half-life of aspirin is about twenty minutes. Flying is permissible while taking aspirin as long as the condition for which the aspirin is taken does not preclude flying and there are no adverse side effects from the aspirin (e.g., stomach discomfort).

Generic name: *aluminum acetate*
Synonym: *Burow's solution*
Usual use: as a wet dressing applied externally

Aluminum acetate, applied as a wet dressing or as an ointment, is used to treat minor skin irritations, eczema, and dry scaly skin. It may also be used to treat certain minor infections of the external ear.

Significant adverse side effects are rarely cited. It is safe to fly while using Burow's solution or a comparable ointment or lotion.

Generic name: *aluminum hydroxide*
Multi-ingredient drugs: Algemol, Almox, Alternagel, Aludrox, Amphogel, Camalox, Decogen, Delcid, Escot, Gaviscon, Gaysal, Gelusil, Kengesin, Kolantyl, Kudrox, Maalox, Mygel, Mylanta, Simeco
Usual dose: (varies)

Aluminum hydroxide, in combination with magnesium hydroxide and other substances, is used to relieve stomach discomfort. It is used in liquid or tablet form. These preparations relieve pain or discomfort associated with too much stomach acid, heartburn, or peptic ulcers.

Products containing aluminum hydroxide do not cause adverse side effects of interest to a pilot, although sometimes a person taking them may develop constipation. A peptic ulcer if active or clinically significant may preclude safe flight.

In general, pilot duties are permissible when aluminum hydroxide is taken. Consult an AME if in doubt about the underlying condition and its effect on safe flight duties.

Generic name: *amcinonide*
Brand name: *Cyclocort*
Usual dose: (applied externally)

Amcinonide is a member of the steroid group. It is used to treat skin that is itchy, inflamed, or irritated. It is applied as a cream to the affected area two or three times a day.

Sometimes minor adverse side effects may occur. They include burning sensations, dryness, or irritation.

The half-life of amcinonide varies because it depends on how much is absorbed through the skin. Flying is permissible while using amcinonide, providing that the underlying condition is not too extensive.

Generic name: *calcium carbonate*
Multi-ingredient drugs: Adeflor-M, Fluornatal, Iron-Ore, Lactocal F., Materna 1-60, Nu-Natal, Pramilet FA, Pramocon, Preobyn, Theraham-M
Usual dose: .5–2 gm as needed

Calcium carbonate, sometimes an ingredient in vitamin-mineral supplements, is commonly used to relieve various kinds of stomach distress. It is used to treat peptic ulcers, stomach irritation, excess stomach acid, heartburn, and indigestion.

Adverse side effects resulting from calcium carbonate are unusual. The possibility of diarrhea or constipation is present but minimal.

The site of the medicinal effect of calcium carbonate is generally the digestive tract. The half-life varies widely depending on how the medication is taken and other factors.

Flying is generally permissible while using calcium carbonate, depending upon the severity of the symptoms being treated. If in doubt, consult an AME.

Generic name: *candicidin*
Brand names: *Candeptin, Vanobid*
Usual dose: 6 mg per day

Candicidin is an antifungus agent. It is used to treat microbial infections of the vagina caused by fungi. It is used either as a tablet inserted in the vagina or as an ointment applied by an applicator.

Adverse side effects are unusual and mild. Sometimes the drug may produce some local irritation.

Candicidin exerts its antibiotic effect at the site of application, and flying is generally permissible while using it.

Generic name: *cantharidin*
Brand name: *Cantharone*
Usual dose: (applied externally)

Cantharidin is used to remove various kinds of warts. It comes in a special solvent that evaporates quickly and leaves the cantharidin in a thin film directly on the wart to be removed.

Cantharidin is a potent blistering agent when applied to normal skin. It is important that it be applied carefully to the wart only, allowed to form a thin film, and, in most instances, then covered.

Since cantharidin is applied externally, its duration of action can be seen directly.

Cantharidin treatment usually will not preclude pilot duties. If the wart is on the sole of the foot or on the palm of the hand, and if the treated wart area becomes excessively reactive, flight duties should be postponed until the area improves.

When in doubt about pilot duties consult an AME.

Generic name: *casanthranol*
Multi-ingredient drugs: Bu-Lax Plus, Comfolax-Plus, Dialose Plus, Diocto-Cas, Dio-Lax Plus, Doctase, Peri-Colace, Sofflax, Stimulax
Usual dose: 30–60 mg per day

Casanthranol is a mild laxative used to relieve constipation. Often, it is used in combination with the stool softener, dioctyl sodium sulfosuccinate. Casanthranol stimulates the movement of the muscles of the bowel and the stool softener allows for easier passage.

Adverse side effects may occur, but they are mild and infrequent. Sometimes the use of combination products containing casanthranol may cause diarrhea, nausea, or abdominal discomfort.

It is usually permissible to fly while taking a casanthranol-containing product, but prior approval by an AME may be advisable. This would be the case if the constipation is severe or prior experience with the laxative indicates a possible marked effect.

Generic name: *ephedrine*
Multi-ingredient drugs: Aladrine, Anasma, Asmex, Asthmalynn, Atromal, Azma-Aid, Barfedrine, Bronchobid, Broncholate, Broncidex, Bronkotabs, Bron Sed, Deltasmyl, Ectasule Minus, Efed, Ephenyllin, Eponal G, Fedrinal, Fedrital, Hydroxyzine Compound, Isabade, Isolate Compound, Isonol, Isophed, Isucom, Kedral, Lardet, Marax, Mudrane GG, Orbidrol, Panaphyllin, Protenol, Quadrinal, Quakedrin, Sudolin, Tedral, TEP Compound, Tepco, Thalfed, Theophed, Theophenyllin, Theoprel, Theosma, Theotal, Verequad, Vitaphen
Usual dose: (varies)

Ephedrine is used to shrink swollen nasal membranes and to open constricted breathing passages, making breathing easier. Hay fever or a cold could be the underlying problem.

In addition to its desired therapeutic effects, ephedrine may cause adverse side effects. These side effects are usually mild or infrequent. Examples of side effects that are of interest to pilots include rapid heartbeat and nervousness.

The half-life of ephedrine is about two hours. It takes eight hours to clear it from the body after the last dose.

It is normally permissible to continue flight duties while using an ephedrine-containing preparation. If the underlying problem is too severe, flight should not be undertaken. If in doubt, consult an AME.

Generic name: *ferrous fumarate*
Brand names: (many)
Multi-ingredient drugs: (many)
Usual dose: 100–400 mg per day

Ferrous fumarate is a source of iron used to treat anemia caused by iron deficiency. It is also a commonly used dietary supplement. It may be taken alone or with supplemental vitamins and other minerals.

In addition to its desired antianemia effect, ferrous fumarate may give rise to undesired side effects. These are infrequent, however, and mild. Sometimes there may be stomach discomfort, diarrhea, or constipation.

Flight duties may be continued safely while taking ferrous fumarate provided that the anemia for which it is taken is not clinically significant. A physician must be consulted in individual cases of anemia to determine the extent of anemia and the actual underlying cause (possible internal bleeding). Supplemental dietary iron taken as a preventive is not a hazard to safe flight.

Generic name: *ferrous gluconate*
Brand names: (many)
Multi-ingredient drugs: (many)
Usual dose: about 1000–1300 mg per day

Ferrous gluconate is a source of iron used to treat anemias caused by iron deficiency. It is also a commonly used dietary supplement and may be used to prevent, rather than treat, anemia due to iron deficiency. It may be taken by itself or with supplemental vitamins and other minerals.

In addition to its desired antianemia effect, ferrous gluconate may give rise to undesired side effects. Side effects, however, are infrequent and mild. Sometimes there may be stomach discomfort, diarrhea, or constipation.

Flight duties may be continued safely while taking ferrous gluconate (see ferrous fumarate in this chapter for similarly applicable comments on clinically significant anemias).

Generic name: *ferrous sulfate*
Brand names: (many)
Multi-ingredient drugs: (many)
Usual dose: about 500 mg per day

Ferrous sulfate is a source of iron used to treat anemias caused by iron deficiency. It is also a commonly used dietary supplement and may be used to prevent, rather than treat, anemia due to iron deficiency. It may be taken alone or with supplemental vitamins and other minerals.

In addition to its desired antianemia effect, ferrous sulfate may give rise to undesired side effects. These are infrequent and mild, however. Sometimes there may be stomach discomfort, diarrhea, or constipation.

Flight duties may be continued safely while taking ferrous sulfate unless an anemia for which it is taken is clinically significant. In this case, a physician must be consulted (see ferrous fumarate in this chapter for similarly applicable comments on clinically significant anemias).

Generic name: *folic acid*
Brand names: (many)
Multi-ingredient drugs: (many)
Usual dose: .1–1 mg per day

Folic acid is a member of the B-complex group of vitamins. It is used to treat certain ailments that arise from a deficiency of folic acid, either because there is too little in the diet or because it is not being absorbed adequately. Folic acid deficiency can cause damage to the nervous system.

The occurrence and severity of unwanted side effects from folic acid are low. Folic acid may mask certain symptoms of pernicious anemia arising from lack of vitamin B_{12}.

Flight duties may be continued while taking folic acid.

Generic name: *guaifenesin*
Synonym: *glyceryl guaiacolate*
Brand names: (many)
Multi-ingredient drugs: (many)
Usual dose: up to 1200 mg per day

Guaifenesin acts to promote the removal of mucus that collects in the throat. It helps coughing remove fluids that may collect in the breathing passages.

Although guaifenesin seldom causes adverse side effects, some do occur from time to time. Examples of these side effects are nervousness, restlessness, headache, and nausea.

It is safe to continue flight activities while using guaifenesin if the side effects have not occurred. It may be that the cold or the respiratory tract malady, if severe, may have a greater effect on one's flying ability than the guaifenesin. In this case the illness itself will preclude flight duties.

Generic name: *haloprogin*
Brand name: *Halotex*
Usual dose: (applied externally)

Haloprogin is applied to the skin either as a cream or as a solution. It is used to treat a variety of fungal infections on the skin.

In some instances haloprogin may give rise to adverse side effects in addition to its desired medicinal effects. Unwanted side effects are usually infrequent and mild. They may include burning, local irritation, itching, or even formation of small blisters.

It is permissible to continue flight duties while using haloprogin. If the adverse side effects do occur, other medications may be available that are also effective.

Generic name: *hexachlorophene*
Multi-ingredient products: Germa Medica, Hexachlor Skin Cleanser, Hexacort, Hexa-Dofscort, Hexagerm, Hyper-Phaze Derma-Surgical, Lanahex, Lavotex, My-Cort, Phisohex, Phisoscrub, Scrubteam Surgical Sponge, Septisol, Soy Dome Cleanser, Surgi Scrub, Wescohex, Westasept, Zemalo Skin Cleanser
Usual dose: (applied to skin)

Hexachlorophene is a component of skin cleansers, used at times as a surgical scrubbing solution or as a prescription skin cleanser.

In addition to its desired effect, hexachlorophene may cause adverse side effects. Usually these are mild or infrequent, appearing more commonly when hexachlorophene is used over a long period of time. An example of one of these side effects that is of interest to pilots is direct irritation of the skin where applied.

It is normally permissible to continue flight activities while using a hexachlorophene preparation. If in doubt, consult an AME.

Generic name: *iodochlorhydroxyquin*
Brand name: *Vioform*
Multi-ingredient drugs: Nystaform, Pedi-Cort V, Racet
Usual dose: (applied externally)

Iodochlorhydroxyquin is used to treat certain kinds of skin inflammation, resulting from eczema, athlete's foot, and other fungal infections.

Although iodochlorhydroxyquin may cause adverse side effects in addition to its desired therapeutic effects, these side effects are usually mild and infrequent. The most common side effect that is seen is irritated skin.

Normally, flight duties while using iodochlorhydroxyquin are permissible. If the condition being treated is too extensive or is seriously infected by bacteria, suspend flight activities and consult an AME.

Generic name: *meclocycline*
Brand name: *Meclan*
Usual dose: (applied externally)

Meclocycline is used in the form of a cream in the treatment of acne. Meclocycline is not absorbed through the skin in detectable amounts. Therefore, the occurrence of side reactions of any kind is unusual. At the site of application of the meclocycline cream, skin irritation may sometimes occur.

Flight activities may be continued while using meclocycline. If skin irritation becomes a problem, discontinue use of the meclocycline to relieve the skin irritation and consult the dermatologist or treating physician.

Generic name: *propylhexedrine*
Brand name: *Benzedrex*
Usual dose: 250 mg

Propylhexedrine is commonly used to relieve a stuffy nose. It is an ingredient of many over-the-counter cold and allergy preparations.

In addition to its desired therapeutic effect, propylhexedrine can cause unwanted side effects. Examples of these side effects that are of significance to pilots include nervousness or restlessness. Usually, side effects are mild and infrequent.

The half-life of propylhexedrine is about three hours. It takes about fifteen hours to clear the substance from the body following the last dose.

Flight duties are permissible if the condition for which the drug is taken is not too severe, if side effects have not occurred, and if a good response to the drug occurs (disappearance of symptoms). If in doubt, consult an AME.

Generic name: *pyridoxine*
Synonym: *vitamin B_6*
Multi-ingredient drugs: (many)
Usual dose: (varies)

Pyridoxine is a vitamin, a member of the B-complex group. Pyridoxine is used to treat persons suspected of having a deficiency. Deficiencies may arise from too little in the diet or from use of B_6-demanding drugs such as isoniazid or oral contraceptives.

37

In addition to its nutritional effect, pyridoxine excess may in rare cases cause unwanted side effects.

It is permissible to continue flight activities while using pyridoxine. If in doubt, consult an AME.

Generic name: *salicylamide*
Multi-ingredient drugs: Arthralgan, Bancap, Codalan, Os-Cal-Gesic, Rhinex, Sinulin
Usual dose: 1000–2000 mg per day

Salicylamide is used to relieve mild pain and to reduce fever. It is an ingredient of many over-the-counter preparations.

In addition to its desired medicinal effects, salicylamide may cause unwanted side effects. Usually these are infrequent and mild. Examples of these side effects that are of significance to pilots include nausea, stomach distress, and drowsiness.

Generally, it is permissible to continue flight activities while using salicylamide. If side effects are felt, it may be prudent to consider some other medication, possibly aspirin or acetaminophen. If the underlying condition being treated is too severe, postpone flying until the condition improves.

Generic name: *testosterone*
Brand names: *Andmone, Ando, Andomone, Andro-Cypionate, Andro-gen, Android T, Androlan, Androlin, Andronaq, Andronate, Aqua-test, Cypo-Testo, Depostomead, Depotest, Dura-Test, Histerone, Lynntestro-Aq, Malestrone, Malogen, Malotrone, Mal-Tron, Manogen, Nendron, Oreton, Pan-Test, Shotest, Tesamone, Testaqua, Testnate, Testoject, Testo-Nate, Testone, Testostal, Testra, Testralate, Testraq, Testromac, Testromed, Thera-Nata, Tos-Dura, Tri-Test*
Usual dose: (varies)

Testosterone is a male hormone. It is used to treat a variety of conditions where masculinizing effects are desired. It also may be used by athletes to build muscle strength. It is sometimes used to treat osteoporosis, a bone-softening condition.

In addition to the desired effects of testosterone there may be rare adverse side effects. These can be quite varied depending on the condition being treated and the amount of testosterone being used. Examples of these that are of significance to pilots include skin rash, sleeplessness, and excitation.

The half-life of testosterone is about ten minutes unless the long-acting form is administered.

Flight duties are permissible when taking testosterone unless the underlying condition for which it is taken precludes safe flight. Each user of testosterone must be evaluated on an individual basis for safety of continued flight activities. Consult an AME when use of testosterone begins.

Generic name: *tetrahydrozoline*
Brand names: *Murine Plus, Tyzine, Visine*
Usual dose: (used as drops)

Tetrahydrozoline is used as a nasal solution to clear congestion in the nose and as an eye solution to treat bloodshot or reddened eyes that may have minor irritations.

In addition to its desired therapeutic effects, tetrahydrozoline may cause unwanted side effects. Usually these effects are mild and infrequent. Examples of these side effects that are of interest to pilots are local burning where applied, sneezing, drowsiness, and lightheadedness.

Usually it is permissible to continue flight activities while using tetrahydrozoline.

The half-life of tetrahydrozoline is about three hours. If untoward effects occur, allow fifteen hours after the last usage of tetrahydrozoline to clear it from the body.

If in doubt about the underlying condition in regard to safe flight, consult an AME.

Generic name: *thiabendazole*
Brand name: *Mintezol*
Usual dose: chewable tablets or suspension

Thiabendazole is used to treat individuals who have parasitic worm infestations. It has been used for nematode infestations as well as trichinosis.

In addition to its desired therapeutic effects, thiabendazole can cause unwanted side effects. Examples of these side effects that may be of significance to pilots include dizziness, nausea, diarrhea, and fatigue.

The severity of the worm infestation is the major factor considered in regard to flight duties. The presence of side effects is another factor. Usually, flight can be continued when thiabendazole is being taken. If in doubt, consult an AME.

Generic name: *undecylenic acid* (and/with *zinc undecylenate*)
Brand names: (many)
Usual dose: (usually a component of a powder or spray)

Undecylenic acid and zinc undecylenate are used separately or together in foot preparations to relieve athlete's foot and to control excessive perspiration.

In addition to their desired therapeutic effect undecylenic acid and zinc undecylenate may cause unwanted side effects. Usually these effects amount to no more than a mild skin irritation, and even this is infrequent.

Flight activities can be continued while using preparations that contain either undecylenic acid or zinc undecylenate or both. If a bothersome side effect occurs, switch to another preparation that lacks these ingredients. If the athlete's foot condition becomes badly infected with bacteria, obtain treatment by a dermatologist and suspend pilot duties until the infection is cleared.

Generic name: *zirconyl hydroxychloride*
Brand names: (many)
Usual dose: (usually a component of a lotion or spray)

Zirconyl hydroxychloride is a common ingredient in many underarm antiperspirant preparations. It is an antiperspirant.

Zirconyl hydroxychloride is one of the safer, least toxic ingredients used in underarm preparations. Side effects are mild and rare. If skin irritation should occur, the problem is relieved by switching to a different preparation with some other antiperspirant ingredient.

Pilots may continue flight activities while using a preparation that contains zirconyl hydroxychloride. It has no impact on flight capability. If discomfort or irritation arises, use a different preparation.

Chapter 6

Category II Drugs: Flight Duties Are Permissible with Approval

Flight duties are generally permissible when taking any of the category II drugs, providing an AME or the FAA has given prior approval. Refer to the individual drug listings here for more specific information about a drug's effects on flight activities.

As always, consult an AME or the FAA if any question remains about the advisability of flying while taking one of these drugs.

Generic name: *acetyl sulfisoxazole*
Brand names: *Gantrisin Syrup, Lipo Gantrisin*
Usual dose: 4–8 gm per day

Acetyl sulfisoxazole is an antibacterial drug. It is a tasteless form of sulfisoxazole. It can be used in oral liquids for the treatment of certain infections, usually of the urinary tract.

Like sulfisoxazole, acetyl sulfisoxazole may cause adverse side effects along with its desired therapeutic effect. Examples of these side effects that are of significance to pilots include abdominal pain, nausea, rash, and vomiting.

The drug's half-life is about five hours. It takes twenty-four hours to eventually clear the drug from the body following the last dose of acetyl sulfisoxazole.

If the underlying infection is asymptomatic and not too severe, continued flight activities are permissible while taking this drug, assuming the absence of side effects. Consult an AME in this respect when acetyl sulfisoxazole has been prescribed.

Brand name: *Actifed* (tablets and syrup)
Ingredients: *triprolidine* and *pseudoephedrine*
Usual dose: one tablet or two teaspoonfuls three to four times per day

Actifed tablets and syrup are proprietary products used to treat symptoms associated with hay fever. Actifed allows easier breathing and helps to dry up a runny nose.

41

Along with the desired therapeutic effects, Actifed may give rise to unwanted side effects. Examples of side effects of interest to pilots are sleepiness, dizziness, some loss of coordination, and a thickening of phlegm (mucous secretions) in the nose and throat.

The half-life of pseudoephedrine, an ingredient of Actifed, is about three hours. It takes nine hours to eventually clear the drug from the body after the last dose.

In general, if hay fever or head cold symptoms are severe enough to require treatment, piloting an aircraft during their presence is unwise. If treatment improves the symptoms, the side effects of the treatment may preclude safe flight. Consult an AME about pilot duties in the above circumstances.

Generic name: *amikacin*
Brand name: *Amikin*
Usual dose: (varies)

Amikacin is an antibiotic, a member of the aminoglycoside group. It is used to treat bacterial infections caused by susceptible organisms.

Although allergic reactions may occur, side effects that would immediately and directly lessen flight skills are quite rare.

The half-life of amikacin is about two hours. It takes about ten hours to eventually clear the drug from the body following the last dose.

The infection being treated may preclude safe pilot duties. Consult an AME about pilot duties if amikacin is prescribed.

Generic name: *amoxicillin*
Brand names: *Amoxil, Larotid, Polymox, Robamox, Sumox, Theda Mox, Trimox*
Usual dose: (varies)

Amoxicillin is an antibiotic, similar to ampicillin. It is used to treat infections caused by certain bacteria.

Along with the desired antibiotic effect, adverse side effects occasionally occur. These include nausea, vomiting, diarrhea, skin rash or hives, and anemia. An allergic reaction may also occur, especially in individuals allergic to penicillin.

The half-life of amoxicillin is one-and-one-half hours. It takes eight hours from the last dose for the drug's eventual clearance from the body.

If the underlying infection is not severe and if there are no significant side effects, flight duties while taking amoxicillin are safe. If in doubt, consult an AME.

Generic name: *ampicillin*
Brand names: *A-Cillin, Alpen, Ambiotic, Amcill-S, Ameri-Cilline, Amphi-Lake, Ampicap-S, Ampichel, Ampicil, Ampico, Ampi-Fort, Ampikin, Ampirex, Amplin, Ancillin, A-Pen, Berla-Pen, Biocillin, Chur-Cillin, Delcillin, Econo-Amp, Extopen, Macill, Marcillin, Megapen, Omnipen, Pen A, Penbritin, Pensyn, Polycillin, Principen, Rancillin, Saramp, Supen, TL-Cillin, Totacillin, Tycil, Vampen, WF Cillin*
Multi-ingredient drugs: Amcill G-C, Polycillin-PRB, Probampacin, Quinamm, Totacillin-PRB
Usual dose: (varies)

Ampicillin is a highly useful and popular antibiotic. It is used to treat infections caused by susceptible microorganisms.

As with other antibiotics, ampicillin may cause a marked sensitivity reaction, sometimes called an allergic reaction. Individuals allergic to penicillin or cephalexin may be allergic to ampicillin as well. Adverse side reactions that may affect persons taking ampicillin include diarrhea, nausea, vomiting, and skin rash.

Generally, it is safe to fly while on ampicillin therapy, but prior consultation with an AME is recommended because the condition being treated may preclude safe flight.

The half-life of ampicillin is about ninety minutes. If flying is suspended, allow one day between the last dose and the resumption of flying.

Generic name: *benzonatate*
Brand name: *Tessalon*
Usual dose: 300 mg per day

Benzonatate is used to stop coughing. The tablets should be swallowed whole, not chewed or allowed to dissolve in the mouth.

Although adverse side effects may occur, they are usually mild and of short duration. Examples of side effects of significance to pilots include headache, mild dizziness, stuffy nose, and nausea.

The half-life of benzonatate is estimated to be eight hours. It takes one day from the last dose for the drug's eventual clearance from the body.

Flying may be permissible while taking benzonatate if the cause of the underlying cough does not preclude safe pilot duties. Consult an AME in this respect.

Generic name: *betamethasone*
Brand names: *Benisone, Celestone, Diprosone, Flurobate, Uticort, Valisone*
Usual dose: (varies)

Betamethasone is a member of the steroid group and is applied as a cream, ointment, lotion, or aerosol. It is used to treat skin inflammations and other similar problems that respond to drugs in the cortisone family.

Just as its uses are quite varied, adverse side effects due to betamethasone can also vary widely. Examples of these side effects that are of interest to pilots include elevated blood pressure, mental depression, psychotic symptoms, ulcer development, and the accumulation of fluids in tissues.

The half-life of betamethasone is about two hours. It takes ten hours from the last dose for the drug to be essentially cleared from the body, although its effects may persist for weeks afterward.

Consult an AME about future flight duties when betamethasone has been prescribed.

Generic name: *bisacodyl*
Brand names: *Bisco-Lax, Dulcolax, Orlax*
Multi-ingredient drugs: Bisolax, Clysodrast
Usual dose: 10–15 mg

Bisacodyl is a laxative. It is used to relieve constipation. It also is used for preoperative preparation as well as for preparation to undergo rectal examination.

Adverse side effects with bisacodyl are usually limited to abdominal cramps and/or diarrhea.

Suspend flight duties when diarrhea occurs as a result of bisacodyl. Consult an AME if in doubt in regard to an adequate recovery from the effects of the diarrhea.

Generic name: *bromelains*
Brand name: *Ananase*
Usual dose: 200,000 units per day

"Bromelains" is a preparation of a group of enzymes used to relieve the symptoms of inflammation and swelling that can accompany injuries and certain surgical procedures.

Although some adverse side effects may occur with the use of bromelains, they are infrequent and mild enough to be of little concern.

Flight duties may be continued while using bromelains if prior approval by an AME is obtained. The effects of the medical procedure that requires use of bromelains may be an important factor in continuing or suspending flying.

Generic name: *brompheniramine*
Brand names: *Allertane, Bromatine, Dimetane, Rolabromophen, Spentane, Steraphenate*
Multi-ingredient drugs: Bromphenate, Cortane, Cortapp, Normatane, Thedabrom, Tri-Phen, Tritane
Usual dose: (varies)

Brompheniramine is an antihistamine, useful for treating hay fever or head cold symptoms. It is useful in providing relief from minor allergic discomforts, including irritated eyes or itching skin.

In addition to its desired therapeutic action, brompheniramine may also cause unwanted side effects. Examples of commonly occurring side effects that are of significance to pilots are drowsiness, dizziness, and lessened coordination.

Suspend flight activities when it is necessary to use brompheniramine. Consideration must be given to the effects of the condition being treated as well as to the side effects of the drug.

Allow one day after drug discontinuation for its clearance from the body. If in doubt, consult an AME in regard to flight duties.

Generic name: *carbenicillin*
Brand names: *Geocillin, Pyopen*
Usual dose: .7–3 gm per day

Carbenicillin is an antibiotic, a member of the penicillin group. It is used to treat certain bacterial infections, especially in the urinary tract.

In addition to its intended antibiotic effect, carbenicillin may cause

45

adverse side effects. Individuals allergic to this antibiotic or to penicillin must use a different drug. Other side effects of interest to pilots include nausea, vomiting, skin rash, and diarrhea.

Flight duties should be suspended while taking carbenicillin. Consult an AME in regard to flying when ill enough to require carbenicillin treatment. The half-life of carbenicillin is one hour. Allow an overnight wait following the last dose of the drug before resuming flight duties.

Generic name: *cefadroxil*
Brand name: *Duricef*
Usual dose: 2000 mg per day

Cefadroxil is an antibiotic, a member of the cephalosporin group. It is used to treat certain urinary tract infections caused by susceptible bacteria.

As with many other antibiotics, strong sensitivity reactions may occur. Individuals allergic to penicillin may react strongly to cefadroxil. Other adverse side reactions that are of significance to pilots, such as diarrhea, nausea, or vomiting, may occasionally occur.

The safety of flying while taking cefadroxil must be judged on an individual basis. The decision is based on the severity of the condition being treated, the side effects of the cefadroxil, and the clinical course of the disease. Consult an AME about pilot duties when treated with cefadroxil.

Generic name: *cephalexin*
Brand name: *Keflex*
Usual dose: 1–4 gm per day

Cephalexin is an antibiotic taken by mouth. Cephalexin can be used for certain infections of the respiratory tract, the ear, the skin, and other regions.

As with many antibiotics, some individuals are allergic to cephalexin. Those who are sensitive to penicillin are often sensitive to cephalexin, even though they may never have taken it before.

In addition to sensitivity reactions, cephalexin may give rise to adverse side effects of significance to pilots. These side effects include diarrhea, nausea, vomiting, sour stomach, and pain in the abdomen.

Consult with an AME about piloting while on cephalexin. The condition for which it is prescribed may preclude safe piloting duties.

The half-life of cephalexin is about two hours. One day after ceasing use, the body is essentially cleared of the drug.

Generic name: *chloramphenicol*
Brand names: *Amphicol, Chloromycetin, Chlortropic, Econochlor, Mychel, Ophthochlor*
Multi-ingredient drugs: Chloromixin, Chlortropic-P, Ophthocort
Usual dose: about 3 gm per day

Chloramphenicol is an antibiotic. It is used to treat certain microbial infections that may be in various parts of the body, including the eyes and ears.

People who are highly sensitive to chloramphenicol may react severely. A substitute antibiotic must then be used.

In addition to its intended antibiotic effect, chloramphenicol can give rise to adverse side reactions. Examples of interest to fliers are nausea, vomiting, diarrhea, headache, and mental confusion. Suppression of the bone marrow, especially the red blood cells, can occur.

Consult an AME about piloting when on chloramphenicol. The condition being treated may preclude safe flight.

The half-life of chloramphenicol is about nine hours. If flying is suspended, allow two days between the last dose and the resumption of flying.

Generic name: *chloroquine*
Brand name: *Aralen*
Usual dose: (varies)

Chloroquine is used to treat malaria or may be taken to prevent malaria. It is effective against many kinds of malaria, but some strains are resistant. Chloroquine may also be used to treat amoebic infestations.

Chloroquine may cause adverse side effects along with its antimalarial effect. Vision may be affected. These visual defects (multiple tiny retinal blind spots) may persist for a time after treatment cessation. Other adverse effects of interest to pilots include headache, nausea, vomiting, and diarrhea.

The half-life of chloroquine is about seven days. It takes three weeks to clear most of the drug from the body.

Continuation of flight duties while taking chloroquine may be allowed, provided an AME gives approval.

Generic name: *chlorpheniramine*
Brand names: *Chlor-Amine, Chlor-Hab, Chlorphenist, Chlor-Trimeton, Fera-TD, Hi-Chlor, Histaron, Histine, Histol, Phenetron*
Multi-ingredient drugs: Alamine, Chlorhistine, Forcold, Histalet Forte, Isclor, Omni-Tuss, Pericol, Sinaprel
Usual dose: 16–24 mg per day

Chlorpheniramine is an antihistamine. It is used to treat symptoms of hay fever such as runny nose, irritation of the eye, certain kinds of skin rash, and other symptoms.

In addition to its desired medicinal effects chlorpheniramine gives rise to adverse side effects. Examples that are of significance to pilots include drowsiness, dizziness, lessened coordination, rash, headache, and stomach distress.

In general, do not fly while taking chlorpheniramine. If one takes the drug under certain circumstances, however, such as only after a flight or at night before going to bed, the AME or FAA may allow a period of treatment without grounding. The half-life of chlorpheniramine is about six hours. To assure significant clearance from the body, allow at least eighteen hours between the last dose and the resumption of flying. Five half-lives, or thirty hours, provide almost total clearance from the body.

Beware of long-acting preparations of chlorpheniramine that may produce drowsiness during the period of flight. There is also a hangover effect during the latter metabolic phases of drug action (in this case in the sixth to twelfth hours). Alcohol and hypoxia may aggravate the drowsiness side effect, especially in flight above eight thousand feet mean sea level.

Generic name: *chlortetracycline*
Brand name: *Aureomycin*
Usual dose: 1–2 gm per day

Chlortetracycline is an antibiotic, a member of the tetracycline group. Chlortetracycline was the first member of this group to be discovered. It is used for a variety of microbial infections.

Like other antibiotics, chlortetracycline may cause a severe sensitivity reaction in some people. For example, severe nausea may be a problem. People known to have a sensitivity to chlortetracycline must use a different antibiotic. Generally, a person sensitive to one member of the tetracycline group is sensitive to the other members of the group.

48

The most common adverse side effects of chlortetracycline involve the stomach and digestive tract. Effects of interest to fliers include a burning sensation in the upper abdomen or stomach, nausea, vomiting, and diarrhea.

Flying while taking chlortetracycline is permissible if the condition for which it is being taken does not preclude safe flight. Consult with an AME in each case.

The half-life of chlortetracycline is about nine hours. If flying is suspended, allow two days between the last dose of chlortetracycline and the resumption of flying. Never take outdated tetracycline. It can cause kidney damage with serious consequences.

Generic name: *clemastine*
Brand name: *Tavist*
Usual dose: (varies)

Clemastine is an antihistamine. It is used to relieve symptoms associated with hay fever, such as runny nose, itchiness, and tearing eyes.

Along with its desired medicinal effects, clemastine may cause unwanted side effects. The most serious of these side effects is drowsiness, which occurs frequently. There may be other side effects, such as dizziness or lessened mental alertness.

Flight activities while taking clemastine are not advisable. Prior approval by an AME or the FAA may be obtained, however, if, during an allergic period, the drug is taken prior to going to bed (by 10 P.M.) and flying is not undertaken until well into the next morning.

Generic name: *clindamycin*
Brand name: *Cleocin*
Usual dose: .6–1.2 gm per day

Clindamycin is an antibiotic used to treat certain infections of the respiratory tract, abdomen, skin, and other regions.

In addition to its medicinal effect, clindamycin may cause side effects, which are sometimes quite serious. Some people are very sensitive to this drug, and another antibiotic must be used. People sensitive to lincomycin may well be sensitive to clindamycin. Side effects that may be of interest to pilots include diarrhea, abdominal pain, and fever.

The condition being treated may preclude safe flight as a pilot. Consult an AME concerning flight duties.

The half-life of clindamycin is about two-and-one-half hours. If flying is suspended, allow one day between the last dose of clindamycin and the resumption of pilot duties, assuming recovery has occurred from the infection requiring treatment.

Generic name: *cloxacillin*
Brand names: *Cloxapen, Tegopen*
Usual dose: 1000–2000 mg per day

Cloxacillin is an antibiotic, a member of the penicillin group. It is used to treat bacterial infections caused by microbes susceptible to cloxacillin.

Like other antibiotics, cloxacillin may cause adverse side effects or an allergic reaction in addition to its intended antimicrobial effect. Individuals allergic to penicillin may be allergic to cloxacillin.

Flight duties may be continued in most instances while using cloxacillin, provided the infection being treated is not too severe. Prior approval by an AME is needed in order to fly with safety.

Generic name: *colistin*
Brand name: *Coly-Mycin S*
Usual dose: (varies)

Colistin is an antibiotic. It is most commonly used to treat certain kinds of bacterial diarrheas in children, but it may be used to treat certain kinds of digestive tract infections in adults.

Generally, adverse side effects do not accompany the use of colistin. It is taken as an oral liquid and acts within the digestive tract contents. Little, if any, is absorbed from the digestive system.

It is safe to continue flying while taking colistin, provided the diarrheal symptoms have abated and the body is not depleted of fluid and salts. Prior approval by an AME is needed. If flying is suspended, consult with the AME concerning the return to flying after the use of colistin is ended.

Generic name: *collagenase*
Brand name: *Santyl*
Usual dose: (applied externally)

Collagenase is an enzyme preparation used as an ointment. It promotes the healing of skin ulcers or burns. It breaks down dead tissue at the injured site, enhancing cleaning of the area and assisting the healing process.

Adverse side effects are usually not a problem with collagenase. If the collagenase preparation is applied to the intact skin surrounding the area being treated, there may be some reddening of the normal skin.

Whether or not flying should be continued while using collagenase is decided on an individual basis. It depends on the nature, the severity, and the extent of injury to the area being treated with collagenase. Consult with an AME about the effects on flight activities.

Generic name: *cyproheptadine*
Brand name: *Periactin*
Usual dose: 12–16 mg per day

Cyproheptadine is used to treat the symptoms of hay fever, such as runny nose, irritated eyes, and itchiness.

In addition to its intended medicinal effects, cyproheptadine may cause unwanted side effects. Examples of these side effects that are of interest to pilots are sleepiness, dizziness, loss of coordination, and fatigue.

Flying should not be undertaken while on cyproheptadine. Like other antihistamines, cyproheptadine may induce sleepiness. Consult with an AME about the possibility of taking a dose prior to going to bed and being cleared for flight the following day. Watch for an early morning hangover effect, however, and if present, do not fly for six or more hours.

Generic name: *demeclocycline*
Brand name: *Declomycin*
Multi-ingredient drug: Declostatin
Usual dose: 600 mg per day

Demeclocycline is an antibiotic, a member of the tetracycline group. It is used to treat infections caused by bacteria and certain other microbes.

An individual sensitive to demeclocycline must use a different antibiotic. Because a person sensitive to demeclocycline is highly likely to be sensitive to the other members of the tetracycline group, a different class of antibiotic should be sought.

Adverse effects of interest to pilots include nausea, vomiting, difficulty in swallowing, and skin rash.

The half-life of demeclocycline is estimated to be about sixteen hours. Flying is probably safe while taking demeclocycline, but approval of an AME is needed to assure that the condition for which the antibiotic is taken does not preclude safe flight. Allow two days between the last dose and the resumption of flying.

Generic name: *desonide*
Brand name: *Tridesilon*
Usual dose: (applied externally)

Desonide is used to assist in the treatment of certain skin problems and for use in the external ear canal. It is applied to the skin as an ointment or cream and used in the ear as a liquid, applied in drops.

In addition to its desired medicinal effects, desonide may cause unwanted side effects. Examples of these side effects that are of interest to pilots include burning sensations, itching, irritation, and dryness.

Whether or not flying can safely be continued while using desonide must be determined on an individual basis. Some of the factors that must be considered are the nature of the problem, the extent of the area being treated, and the response of the individual to the treatment. Consult with an AME about the safety of flight activities while using desonide.

Generic name: *desoximetasone*
Brand name: *Topicort*
Usual dose: (applied externally)

Desoximetasone, a cortisone-type drug, is used in the form of an ointment to treat certain kinds of skin conditions, especially inflammations. It is applied directly to the affected area of the skin.

In addition to its desired medicinal effects, it may give rise to some adverse side effects. Examples of these side effects that are of interest to pilots include a burning feeling, itchiness, irritation, and dryness.

Whether or not flying can be safely continued while using desoximetasone must be determined on an individual basis. Some of the factors that will be considered are the nature of the problem, the extent of the affected area, and the general condition of the individual. Consult with an AME about the safety of flight activities while using desoximetasone.

Generic name: *desoxyribonuclease and fibrinolysin*
Brand name: *Elase*
Usual dose: (applied externally)

Desoxyribonuclease and fibrinolysin comprise a preparation of two enzymes, or a group of enzymes, that assist in cleaning and consequently healing certain kinds of wounds. These include skin ulcers and burns.

In addition to its desired effects, desoxyribonuclease-fibrinolysin may cause adverse side effects. The side effects, however, are usually infrequent and mild. Examples of some of these side effects that are of interest to pilots are fever, itchiness and irritation in the treated area, and a possible burning sensation.

It is generally permissible to fly while using desoxyribonuclease and fibrinolysin. Prior approval by an AME is wise because the nature of the condition being treated may preclude safe flight.

Generic name: *dexbrompheniramine and pseudoephedrine*
Brand names: *Dehist, Disophrol, Drixoral, Histodrix*
Usual dose: Two dosage units per day

Dexbrompheniramine and pseudoephedrine are used together for the treatment of symptoms caused by hay fever, especially a stuffy nose.

In addition to their desired medicinal effects, dexbrompheniramine and pseudoephedrine may give rise to unwanted side effects. Examples of these side effects that are of interest to pilots include drowsiness, loss of alertness, and confusion.

Flight duties may be all right while using dexbrompheniramine and pseudoephedrine, but prior permission should be obtained from an AME. If flying is suspended, allow at least twenty-four hours between the last dosage unit and the resumption of flight activities.

Generic name: *dexchlorpheniramine*
Brand name: *Polaramine*
Usual dose: Two dosage units per day

Dexchlorpheniramine is an antihistamine. It is commonly used to treat the allergic symptoms of hay fever, hives, various skin irritations, reactions to insect bites, and runny nose.

As with other antihistamines, dexchlorpheniramine may cause adverse side effects in addition to its desired medicinal effects. Examples of these side effects that are of interest to pilots are drowsiness (which may not be apparent), dizziness, nausea, and headache.

Flight duties should not be conducted while using dexchlorpheniramine, but if an evening dose is taken at bedtime, an AME may give approval for flying on the next day. If flying is suspended, allow at least twenty-four hours between the last dose and the resumption of flying.

Generic name: *dicloxacillin*
Brand names: *Dicill, Dynapen, Pathocil, Veracillin*
Usual dose: 500–1000 mg per day

Dicloxacillin is an antibiotic, a member of the penicillin group. It is readily absorbed from the digestive tract and is available in a form to be taken by mouth. Dicloxacillin is effective against some strains of microbes that are resistant to other forms of penicillin.

In addition to its desired antibiotic effect dicloxacillin may cause adverse side effects. The most serious side effects that pilots need to consider are allergic reactions and effects on the digestive tract. These may lead to nausea, vomiting, skin rash, hives, and itchiness and swelling of the fingers, toes, and face.

It is permissible to fly while taking dicloxacillin if the condition for which it is taken does not preclude safe flight. Consult an AME for a decision in each case.

Generic name: *diflorasone*
Brand name: *Florone*
Usual dose: (applied externally)

Diflorasone is a member of the corticosteroid group. It is used to treat the inflammation, itchiness, and redness of certain skin conditions.

In addition to its desired medicinal effects, diflorasone may cause certain unwanted side effects. The strength of the side effects depends on the size of the area to which the diflorasone is applied, and at times, how the affected area is dressed. Some of the side effects that may occur are burning, itching, and irritation.

It may be permissible to continue flight activities while using diflorasone, if an AME so indicates. If flying is suspended, check with the AME about when it is safe to return to flying.

Generic name: *dimethindene*
Brand names: *Forhistal, Triten*
Usual dose: 2.5–5 mg per day

Dimethindene is used to treat the symptoms of allergic hay fever. It is an antihistamine and helps with runny nose, eye irritation, and rash or itchiness of the skin.

In addition to its desired medicinal effects, dimethindene may cause adverse side effects, including drowsiness and decreased mental alertness.

54

It may not be safe to fly an airplane, drive a car, or operate dangerous machinery.

Suspend flight activities while taking dimethindene. (The condition being treated may preclude safe piloting as well.) When use of dimethindene is ended, twelve hours following discontinuation of treatment should see virtually full clearance of the drug from the body.

Consult an AME if the medication is taken in small amounts and only at night, because flight duties the following day may be permissible under certain circumstances.

Generic name: *diphenhydramine*
Brand names: *Benadryl, Benahist, Ben-Allergin, Benoject, Cumbedryl, Dihydrex, Fenylhist, Hyrexin, Lynnodryl, Midryl, Pardril, Phenadrine, Phenamin, Premodril, Tegadryl, Truxadryl*
Usual dose: 150–200 mg per day

Diphenhydramine is an antihistamine. It is used to relieve the symptoms of hay fever, such as runny nose, irritated eyes, and a rash or itchy skin. It may also relieve the effects of motion sickness.

In addition to its desired medicinal effects, it may also cause adverse side reactions. Because drowsiness and reduced mental alertness are possible side effects, users of diphenhydramine may not be able to safely pilot an airplane, drive a car, or operate heavy machinery. Other side effects of significance to pilots may include impaired coordination, blurred vision, and distressed or painful upper abdomen.

Suspend flying while taking diphenhydramine. The half-life of diphenhydramine is about eight hours, and at least twenty-four hours should be allowed between the last dose of diphenhydramine and the resumption of flight activities. Consult an AME if the medication is taken in small amounts only prior to going to bed, because flying the following morning may be permissible.

Generic name: *diphenoxylate*
Brand names: *Di-Atro, Diphenatol, Dirid, Enoxa, Lofene, Logen, Lomanate, Lomotil, Lonox*
Usual dose: 20 mg per day

Diphenoxylate is used to stop diarrhea, whether infectious or due to other causes, including use of alcohol. Because of the close chemical resemblance of diphenoxylate to meperidine, a less-than-therapeutic dose of atropine is combined to avert taking an overdose of diphenoxylate.

In addition to the antidiarrheal effects of diphenoxylate, unwanted side effects may occur. Examples of side effects that are of interest to pilots include dizziness, drowsiness, headache, and nausea.

Under certain circumstances a pilot may continue flight activities while taking diphenoxylate, but prior approval by an AME must be obtained. The half-life of diphenoxylate is about fourteen hours. If flying is suspended, allow at least two days between the last dose and the resumption of flying. If possible, a three-day interval is preferable. The diarrhea that required treatment may have caused serious dehydration and salt loss from the body, and both of these conditions can represent flight hazards (especially decreased tolerances to G forces).

Generic name: *diphenylpyraline*
Brand names: *Beldin, Diafen, Hispril, Ristadil*
Usual dose: 10 mg per day

Diphenylpyraline is an antihistamine, useful for treating allergic hay fever and runny nose. It is also useful for relieving minor allergic discomforts such as irritated eyes or itchy skin.

In addition to its desired therapeutic effects, diphenylpyraline may also cause unwanted side effects. Examples of more commonly occurring side effects that are of interest to pilots are drowsiness, dizziness, and impaired coordination. While using diphenylpyraline it may be unsafe to pilot an aircraft, drive a car, or operate dangerous machinery.

Suspend flight duties while taking diphenylpyraline. When use of diphenylpyraline is ended safe flight duties can be undertaken, in general, twelve hours later. Consult an AME if the drug is taken only prior to going to bed. Flight the next day may be permissible if the dose taken upon retiring is relatively low (5 mg).

Generic name: *doxycycline*
Brand names: *Doxychel, Vibramycin*
Usual dose: 100 mg per day

Doxycycline is an antibiotic, a member of the tetracycline group. It is used to treat many different kinds of infections that are caused by microbes deemed especially susceptible to doxycycline.

In a few instances doxycycline will cause a sharp sensitivity reaction. People who are sensitive to doxycycline must use a different antibiotic. Also, a person sensitive to doxycycline is probably sensitive to the other members of the tetracycline group.

In addition to its desired antibiotic effect, doxycycline may cause some adverse side effects. Examples of adverse side effects of interest to pilots include nausea, vomiting, diarrhea (rarely), and skin rashes.

Consult an AME about flying while taking doxycycline. The condition for which it is taken may preclude safe flight.

The half-life of doxycycline is about fifteen hours. If flying is suspended while taking doxycycline, allow two days between the last dose and the resumption of flying.

Generic name: *erythromycin*

Brand names: *Amysin, Bristamycin, Dowmycin E, E-Biotic, Econo-Mycin, E-Mycin, Erythroban, Erythrocin, Ilosone, Ilotycin, Kesso-Mycin, Pediamycin, Robimycin, Sanmycin, Steromycin, Theramycin, Van-Mycin*

Usual dose: 1–4 gm per day

Erythromycin is an antibiotic used to treat a variety of infectious ailments caused by susceptible microorganisms.

As with other antibiotics, erythromycin can give rise to a severe reaction in those who are very sensitive. When an individual knows from past experience that the erythromycin might cause a strong reaction, another antibiotic must be used.

Adverse effects that are of interest to pilots are abdominal cramps and discomfort, nausea, vomiting, and diarrhea. Skin rash can occur. Higher doses often are more likely to produce adverse side effects.

The half-life of erythromycin is estimated to be about five hours. Flying is compatible with ingested erythromycin if an AME approves, but the condition for which it is taken may preclude safe flying. If flying is suspended, allow one-and-one-half days between the last dose and resumption of flying.

Generic name: *ethaverine*

Brand names: *Am-Thav, Cebral, Circubid, Eta-Lent, Ethabid, Ethaquin, Ethatab, Ethavabid, Ethavas, Ethaverol, Ethavex, Ethavid, Isovex, Laverin, Myoquin, Neopavrin, Pava-Span, Paverjec, Spasmatrol*

Multi-ingredient drugs: Espasmon, Opocal, Pasmin, Pavricol

Usual dose: 300 mg per day

Ethaverine is used to treat certain kinds of blood circulation difficulties. It relaxes the smooth muscles of the larger arteries, thus enhancing blood circulation. It can also help to relieve the spastic, or contracted, smooth muscle of the digestive or urinary tract.

In addition to its desired relaxing effects on smooth muscle, ethaverine may cause certain unwanted side effects. Examples of these effects that are of interest to pilots are drowsiness, vertigo (dizziness), nausea, and abdominal distress.

Consult an AME prior to flying with ethaverine. The condition being treated may preclude safe flight.

Generic name: *etidronate*
Brand name: *Didronel*
Usual dose: (varies)

Etidronate is used to treat certain kinds of bone disorders. It may also be used after total hip replacement. It is also used in Paget disease and sometimes after spinal cord injury. Frequently, etidronate is used over a period of many weeks or months.

In addition to its desired medicinal effect, etidronate may cause unwanted side effects. Some of these side effects that may be of significance to pilots are diarrhea, nausea, vomiting, and pain in certain bones.

The feasibility of continued flight activities must be evaluated on an individual basis. The condition for which the drug is prescribed may preclude safe flight duties. Consult an AME in regard to piloting aircraft while on etidronate.

Generic name: *flavoxate*
Brand name: *Urispas*
Usual dose: 600–800 mg per day

Flavoxate acts to relieve muscle spasm in the urinary tract. Generally, it is used to lessen uncomfortable symptoms associated with the urinary tract. Flavoxate gives relief of symptoms but is not a curative agent.

In addition to the desired medicinal effects, flavoxate may give rise to adverse side effects. Examples of these side effects that are of significance to pilots are nausea, vomiting, nervousness, drowsiness, and blurred vision.

Whether or not flight activities can be safely continued while taking flavoxate must be determined on an individual basis. Consult with an

AME about flying while using flavoxate. The condition for which the drug is given may preclude safe flight.

Generic name: *flumethasone*
Brand name: *Locorten*
Usual dose: (applied externally)

Flumethasone is applied to the skin in the form of a cream. It is used to treat certain kinds of skin ailments that respond to steroid-type drugs.

Besides its desirable medicinal effects, flumethasone may cause unwanted side effects. Examples of these side effects that are of special interest to pilots are skin burning, itching, irritation, and dryness. The severity of any side reactions depends on the size of the area to which flumethasone is applied as well as the kind of dressing placed over the area. These factors influence the amount absorbed into the body.

Continued flight activities while using flumethasone will depend upon each individual's circumstances. The condition being treated, the amount of flumethasone absorbed through the skin, and the response of the individual to the drug will determine whether or not pilot duties can be conducted with safety. Consult with an AME in regard to pilot duties when using flumethasone.

Generic name: *fluocinolone*
Brand names: *Fluonid, Synalar, Synemol*
Multi-ingredient drug: Neo-Synalar
Usual dose: (applied externally)

Fluocinolone is applied to the skin, either as a cream, an ointment, or as a solution for use on the skin. These forms of fluocinolone are used to treat certain kinds of skin ailments that respond to steroid-type drugs.

Along with its desirable medicinal effects, fluocinolone may cause unwanted side effects. Examples of these side effects that may be of special significance to pilots are skin irritation, burning, itching, or drying at the site of application of the fluocinolone. The occurrence and the severity of these side reactions depend on the amount of fluocinolone applied to the skin and how the treated area is dressed.

Each user of fluocinolone should consult an AME concerning flight duties. Factors to be considered include the nature of the condition being treated, the amount of fluocinolone used, and the response of the individual to the drug.

Generic name: *fluocinonide*
Brand names: *Lidex, Topsyn*
Usual dose: (applied externally)

Fluocinonide is applied to the skin either as a cream, an ointment, or a gel. These forms of fluocinonide can be used to limit inflammation, stop itching, or relieve certain other kinds of skin problems.

Along with its desirable medicinal effects fluocinonide may cause unwanted side effects. Examples of these side effects that may be of significance to pilots are skin irritation, burning, itching, or drying. These reactions depend on the amount of fluocinonide applied to the skin and how the treated area is dressed.

Users of fluocinonide must be evaluated for flight activity on an individual basis. Consult with an AME about continuing or suspending flight activities while being treated with this drug.

Generic name: *flurandrenolide*
Brand name: *Cordran*
Usual dose: (applied externally)

Flurandrenolide is a steroid-type drug. It is applied externally to the skin for skin problems that may respond to steroid-type medication.

Along with its desired medicinal effects, flurandrenolide may cause undesirable side effects. Examples of these side effects that are of special significance to pilots include burning, itchiness, and drying of the skin. The type and severity of the side effects depend not only on the individual's condition, but also on the amount of flurandrenolide used, the size of the affected area, and the way in which the area is dressed.

Capability to continue flight activities must be judged on an individual basis. Consult an AME about suspending or continuing flying.

Generic name: *halcinonide*
Brand names: *Halciderm, Halog*
Usual dose: (applied externally)

Halcinonide is a steroid-type drug. It is applied to the skin for problems that may respond to steroid-type medications.

Along with its desired therapeutic effects, halcinonide may cause adverse side effects. Examples of these side effects that are of special significance to pilots include skin burning, itching, irritation, and dryness. The nature of the side effects is related to the amount of halcinonide applied, the size of the affected area, and the kind of dressing used.

Consult an AME in regard to undertaking pilot duties while under treatment with halcinonide. In some cases, the condition being treated will preclude safe flight.

Generic name: *hyoscyamine*
Multi-ingredient drugs: Arcolase, Butabell HMB, Cystospaz, Digestamic, Kutrase, Levsin, Levsinex, Prosed, Pyridium Plus, Ru-Tuss, Sidonna, Trac-Tabs, Tri-Cone Plus, Urised
Usual dose: .25–1 mg

Hyoscyamine is used to quiet an overactive digestive tract. The overactivity can be either excessive contractions or excessive secretions. It is used to control peptic ulcers, "nervous stomach," and other hyperactivity states.

In addition to its desired therapeutic effects, hyoscyamine can cause unwanted side effects. Examples of these side effects that are of interest to pilots include dry mouth, visual difficulties, and increased heart rate.

Suspend flight activities while taking hyoscyamine. Consult an AME about a return to flight duties when hyoscyamine has been prescribed.

Generic name: *iodoquinol*
Synonym: *diiodohydroxyquin*
Brand names: *Panaquin, Yodoxin*
Multi-ingredient drugs: Cort-Quin, Lidaform-HC, Vytone
Usual dose: 1950 mg per day

Iodoquinol is used to treat intestinal infestations by amoebae and, with other drugs, to treat certain other ailments of the digestive tract and liver.

In addition to its desired therapeutic effects, iodoquinol may cause unwanted side effects. Examples of these side effects that may be significant to pilots include nausea and vomiting, fever, dizziness, and diarrhea.

Each user of iodoquinol must be evaluated on an individual basis for safety of continued flight activities. Consult with an AME when use of iodoquinol begins. The amoebic infection symptoms may be severe enough (especially if dysentery is present) to preclude pilot duties.

Generic name: *lincomycin*
Brand name: *Lincocin*
Usual dose: 1.5–2 gm per day

Lincomycin is an antibiotic with limited uses. It is used to treat certain kinds of infections that are caused by sensitive microbes. In a few instances an individual can have a serious reaction to lincomycin. Persons known to be very sensitive cannot be given lincomycin or the antibiotic clindamycin, which is chemically similar.

In addition to its desired effect, lincomycin can also give rise to certain side effects in the stomach and remaining digestive tract, the skin, the heart and circulating blood, the liver, and the senses. Examples of adverse effects of significance to pilots include diarrhea, nausea, vomiting, skin rashes, ringing in the ear, and dizziness.

The half-life of lincomycin is about five-and-one-half hours. Eventual clearance of the drug from the body takes about two days.

Consult an AME concerning pilot duties while under treatment. The condition being treated may preclude safe flight.

Generic name: *mafenide*
Brand names: *Sulfamylon, Winthrocine*
Usual dose: (applied externally)

Mafenide is used to assist in the treatment of moderate and serious burns. It is an antiinfective agent, a member of the sulfonamide group.

In addition to its desired therapeutic effects, mafenide may cause adverse side effects. Examples of these side effects that may be of significance to pilots include skin rash, itching, burning, or pain. Some of these effects, however, may be due to the original burn being treated.

Continuation of flight activities while using mafenide must be evaluated on an individual basis. Factors that must be considered include the site of the burn, the extent of the involved area, and the severity of the burn. Consult with an AME about flying while being treated with mafenide. The original injury may preclude safe flight.

Generic name: *mebendazole*
Brand name: *Vermox*
Usual dose: 2 tablets daily for 3 days

Mebendazole is used for treatment of intestinal infestations by whipworms, roundworms, pinworms, or hookworms. If the course of treatment is not effective within three weeks, a second course of treatment is given.

In addition to its desirable medicinal effects, mebendazole may also cause adverse side effects. These side effects are not common and usually do not last very long. Examples include abdominal pain and diarrhea.

Flight activities may be continued while taking mebendazole, but consultation with the FAA should be made prior to doing so.

Generic name: *methacycline*
Brand name: *Rondomycin*
Usual dose: 600 mg per day

Methacycline is an antibiotic, a member of the tetracycline group. It is used to treat infections caused by certain microorganisms.

Persons known to be very sensitive to methacycline must use a different antibiotic. A sensitized person may react sharply if given methacycline or any other member of the tetracycline group.

Adverse reactions of interest to pilots include a sensitivity reaction, difficulty in swallowing, diarrhea, nausea, vomiting, and skin rash.

The half-life of methacycline is estimated to be about sixteen hours. Five days after discontinuing the drug, most of it will be cleared from the body.

Consult an AME concerning pilot duties while taking methacycline. Sometimes the condition under treatment will preclude safe piloting duties.

Generic name: *methandrostenolone*
Brand name: *Dianabol*
Usual dose: 2.5–5 mg per day

Methandrostenolone is a drug with male sex hormone actions. It is used to treat weakened bone conditions such as osteoporosis (a thinning of bone with loss of calcium).

In addition to its desired therapeutic effects, methandrostenolone may cause adverse side effects. Examples of these side effects that may be of interest to pilots include changes in certain secondary sexual characteristics (growth of facial hair in women), nausea, vomiting, and a feeling of fullness.

Each user of methandrostenolone must be evaluated on an individual basis for the safe continuance of flight activities. Consult with an AME. The condition under treatment may preclude safe flight.

The half-life of methandrostenolone is about eighteen hours. It takes about three days after discontinuation of therapy with methandrostenolone to eventually clear it from the body. The masculinizing effects, however, may not disappear for months following discontinuation of the drug.

Generic name: *methenamine*
Brand names: *Hiprex, Maleen, Mandastat, Mandelamine, Mandelex, Mandine, Manese, Methalate, Methavin, Renelate, Urex, Urispec*
Usual dose: 4 gm per day

Methenamine is used for its antibacterial effect in the urinary tract. It is effective in suppressing bacteria that may appear in the urine in a variety of infections.

In addition to its desired antibacterial activity methenamine may cause unwanted side effects. Examples of these side effects that may be of significance to pilots include an upset stomach and, sometimes, a skin rash. These side effects, however, are usually no more than a mild to moderate discomfort.

Flight activities may be continued while using methenamine if an AME gives prior approval.

Generic name: *methyltestosterone*
Brand names: *Android, Arcosterone, Metandren, Oreton Methyl, Testoral, Testred, Theelandrol*
Multi-ingredient drugs: Afrodex, Aphrodac, Basodrex, Estratest, Primotest, Teston, Virilon, Votestone
Usual dose: (varies)

Methyltestosterone is a male sex hormone. It is used for a variety of conditions in men and women.

In addition to its desired medicinal effects, methyltestosterone may cause a wide variety of undesired side effects. Since methyltestosterone is a sex hormone, the side effects often affect secondary sex characteristics. In women the voice may become deeper and facial hair may develop.

Each user of methyltestosterone must be evaluated individually for safety of continued flying. Consult with an AME in regard to flight duties. FAA consultation may be necessary.

64

Generic name: *minocycline*
Brand names: *Minocin, Vectrin*
Usual dose: 200 mg per day

Minocycline is an antibiotic, a member of the tetracycline group. It is used to treat many different kinds of infections caused by susceptible microbes.

Like other antibiotics, minocycline may infrequently give rise to a sharp sensitivity reaction. When this occurs, a different antibiotic must be used. Sensitivity to minocycline probably means that a similar reaction will occur with all other members of the tetracycline group.

Along with its antibiotic effect minocycline may cause adverse side effects. Examples of interest to fliers include difficulty in swallowing, nausea, vomiting, diarrhea, and skin rashes.

It may be safe to fly while taking minocycline, but approval of an AME is needed. The half-life of minocycline is about fifteen hours. If flying is suspended, allow at least three days between the last dose and the resumption of flying.

Generic name: *nalidixic acid*
Brand name: *Neggram*
Usual dose: 4 gm per day

Nalidixic acid is an antibacterial drug used to treat infections of the urinary tract caused by certain microbes.

The intended effect may be accompanied by adverse side effects. Examples of side effects of interest to pilots include nausea, vomiting, diarrhea, skin rash, spinning sensations, and dizziness.

Consult with an AME prior to flying while taking nalidixic acid. The condition being treated may preclude safe flight as a pilot.

The half-life of nalidixic acid is about two hours. If flying is suspended, allow one day between the last dose and resumption of flying.

Generic name: *nitrofurantoin*
Brand names: *Baracin, Cyantin, Furachel, Furalan, Furaloid, Furan, Furantoin, Furarex, Furaton, Furodon, J-Dantin, Macrodantin, Megafuran, Nitrex, Sarodant, Theda-NF, TL-Fura, Trantoin, Van-Dantin*
Usual dose: 200–400 mg per day

Nitrofurantoin is an antibacterial drug used to treat specific infections of the urinary tract that are caused by certain bacteria.

65

In addition to the intended medicinal effects, nitrofurantoin may also give rise to adverse side effects. Examples of side effects that are of interest to pilots include nausea, vomiting, diarrhea, abdominal pain, headache, drowsiness, and fever.

The half-life of nitrofurantoin is about six hours. Consult an AME prior to flying while taking nitrofurantoin. The condition being treated may preclude safe flight. If flying is suspended, allow at least one day between the last dose and the resumption of flying.

Generic name: *nitrofurazone*
Brand names: *Carbazone, Furacin, Furazyme, Nisept, Nitrifur*
Usual dose: (applied externally)

Nitrofurazone is an antibacterial drug that is applied to the surface of moderate to severe burns and to skin grafts. It serves to diminish the development of bacterial contamination of the affected areas.

In addition to its desired antibacterial effect, nitrofurazone may cause adverse side effects. These are infrequent and, when they occur, are usually quite mild. Generally, side effects occur as a skin irritation or an outbreak of hives in or near the treated area.

A burn or skin graft serious enough to require nitrofurazone may adversely affect a pilot's flying ability. Healing of the burn or graft area must determine when resumption of flight activities is possible. This is a matter for AME or FAA consultation.

Generic name: *noscapine*
Brand names: *Airbid, Isofil, Theo-Nar, Tusscapine*
Usual dose: up to 120 mg per day

Noscapine is used to relieve coughing in conditions caused by allergies, colds, flu, and various respiratory ailments.

In addition to its therapeutic cough-suppressing effect, noscapine may cause undesired side effects. Examples of these side effects that are of significance to pilots are drowsiness and nausea. These tend to occur primarily with high doses of the drug.

Under certain circumstances, flight activities may be continued while using noscapine, provided that prior approval by an AME is obtained. The decision is based on the response to treatment, absence of side effects, and the degree of the underlying illness. If flight activities are suspended, consult the AME about resumption of flying after use of noscapine is ended. If the underlying condition is too extensive or severe, grounding will be advised until substantial recovery has occurred.

Generic name: *nystatin*
Brand names: *Mycostatin, Nilstat*
Multi-ingredient drugs: Achrostatin V, Comycin, C-V Statin, Mytrex, Terrastatin, Tetrastatin
Usual dose: (varies)

Nystatin is an antibiotic that is effective against certain kinds of fungal infections. It is sold as an ointment, a powder, and a cream for use on the skin or mucous membranes. It is also sold as vaginal tablets. Nystatin may be taken by mouth in certain preparations for fungal infections of the digestive tract.

Adverse side effects caused by nystatin are usually of little consequence. Skin irritation may occur, and the oral medication may cause some nausea, vomiting, or diarrhea.

Flying is usually permissible while using nystatin, but consultation with an AME should be made beforehand.

Generic name: *oxacillin*
Brand name: *Prostaphlin*
Usual dose: 2000 mg per day

Oxacillin is an antibiotic, often used in the treatment of infections caused by bacteria that are resistant to penicillin.

Although oxacillin may cause adverse side effects along with its desired antibacterial effect, these side reactions are more subtle than apparent. There may be a skin rash or a fever reaction. The most serious response to oxacillin is an allergic reaction.

Consult an AME about flight duties when oxacillin is prescribed. The infection that requires treatment may preclude safe piloting activities until it is adequately controlled.

Generic name: *oxtriphylline*
Brand name: *Choledyl*
Usual dose: about 800 mg per day

Oxtriphylline is used to ease breathing in asthma attacks. It works to open constricted breathing passageways. It may be of use also in certain cases of bronchitis.

In addition to its desired therapeutic effects, oxtriphylline may cause unwanted side effects. Examples of these adverse side effects that are of significance to pilots include headache, rapid heart rate, diarrhea, and restlessness.

The half-life of oxtriphylline is about eleven hours. It takes two days to clear the body of the drug after its use is discontinued.

Each user of oxtriphylline must be evaluated individually to determine if flight activities can be continued with safety while using oxtriphylline. Consult with an AME about continued flying.

Generic name: *oxytetracycline*
Brand names: *Deltamycin, Oxybiocycline, Oxy-Kesso-Tetra, Oxymycin, Oxy-Tetra 250, Terramycin, Tetrachel, Tetramine*
Multi-ingredient drugs: Terrastatin, Urobiotic-250
Usual dose: 1–2 gm per day

Oxytetracycline is an antibiotic, a member of the tetracycline group. It was introduced in 1950, just two years after the first member of the tetracycline group, chlortetracycline. Newer antibiotics may be more effective or safer than oxytetracycline in some instances. It is often used in small, once-daily doses to treat acne.

People sensitive to oxytetracycline must use a different antibiotic. Those who are sensitive to this antibiotic are probably sensitive to other members of the tetracycline group.

In addition to its intended antibiotic effect, some adverse effects may also occur. Examples of adverse side effects of interest to pilots include nausea, vomiting, and diarrhea.

The half-life of oxytetracycline is about nine hours. Flying is often compatible with taking oxytetracycline (especially when used to treat acne). If a severe body infection is present, however, obtain the prior approval of an AME before flying. If flying is suspended, allow at least two days between the last dose and the resumption of flying.

Generic name: *para-aminobenzoate*
Brand name: *Potaba*
Usual dose: (varies)

Para-aminobenzoic acid has many uses. It is considered to be a member of the B-complex group of vitamins. It is used to treat fibrosis, scleroderma (formation of hard, pigmented patches on the skin), and other ailments.

In addition to its desired therapeutic effect, para-aminobenzoate in excess may cause adverse side effects. Examples of these side effects that are of significance to pilots include skin rash, fever, and nausea.

Consult an AME about piloting duties when use of para-aminobenzoate begins. Normally, pilot duties need not be interrupted unless the status of the underlying condition for which it is taken precludes safe flight. If adverse side effects develop, flight must be suspended until they go away after the drug is discontinued.

Generic name: *penicillin G*
Brand names: *Amocillin, Aqua-Cillin, Kay-Cee-Pen, Kesso-Pen, MP-Cillin, Ora-Pen, Oro-Cillin, Pen-Bev, Pentids, Pfizerpen-G, Stanicillin-PO, Sugracillin, Thera-Cillin*
Usual dose: (varies)

Penicillin G (also called penicillin G potassium or potassium penicillin G) was one of the earliest antibiotics, discovered in the 1930s. It is still an important antiinfective drug. It is used to treat certain bacterial infections and, in certain instances, for preventive care. Whether penicillin G or some other antibiotic should be used depends on the cause of the infection. Penicillin G is only effective against certain bacteria; therefore, identification of the bacteria causing the infection is often attempted through culturing of samples.

Penicillin G is a relatively safe drug. Adverse reactions may occur, but they are infrequent and often mild. Some individuals may be very sensitive, in which case another antibiotic must be selected.

The half-life of pure penicillin G is short: one-half hour. Five half-lives reduce the drug level in the body to about 3 percent of its initial level. Consult an AME about flying when treated with penicillin. The infection being treated (for example, a streptococcic sore throat) may preclude flying due to the toxic reaction of the infection. In general, allow two days after successful treatment before returning to flight duties if suspended.

Generic name: *penicillin V*
Brand names: *Acillin-VK, Ben-Bev-V, Betapen VK, Caropen VK, Cocillin VK, Compocillin VK, Cumbercillin-S, Del-Pen VK, Kesso-Pen VK, Lanacillin VK, Ledercillin VK, Marpen-VK, Oro-Cillin VK, Ro-Cillin VK, Theda Pen VK, Uticillin VK, V-Cillin K, Veetids*
Usual dose: (varies)

Penicillin V (also called penicillin V potassium or potassium penicillin V) is an antibiotic used to treat specific bacteria that are not penicillin resistant. Penicillin V is well suited to being taken by mouth. It is also used as a preventive medication under certain conditions.

Penicillin V is safer than most drugs. Adverse reactions occur rarely and often are mild. Some people are very sensitive to penicillin and react strongly to it; in these instances a different antibiotic must be used.

Adverse effects of interest to pilots, except those who are highly sensitive, are few. Use of penicillin V potassium while flying should be approved by an AME, as the condition for which it is taken (infection, for example) may preclude safe flight.

The half-life of penicillin V potassium is one hour. Allow at least one day between the last dose and the resumption of flying if previously suspended due to the illness for which the penicillin is prescribed.

Generic name: *phenolphthalein*
Usual dose: 60–100 mg per day

Phenolphthalein is a popularly used laxative.

In addition to its desired effect, phenolphthalein may cause adverse side effects. Usually, these side effects are mild and infrequent. A skin rash may appear. A greater hazard is diarrhea due to taking more than the prescribed amount.

It is wise to suspend flight activities on the day the phenolphthalein is used. When constipation is no longer a problem and the use of phenolphthalein is ended, pilot duties can be resumed.

Generic name: *phenylephrine*
Brand names: *Degest, Neo-Synephrine*
Multi-ingredient drugs: Ak-cide, Blephamide, Naldec, Ophtaha P/S, Or-Toptic M, Ro Ophto, Sherhist, Tri-Oph, Vasocidin
Usual dose: (varies)

Phenylephrine is used as a decongestant to open up clogged nasal passages that may accompany head colds and other causes of sinus congestion.

In addition to its desired decongestant effect, phenylephrine may cause other undesired effects. Usually these effects do not have a significant impact on the flying capability of an individual. If phenylephrine is used too often as a decongestant, however, a reverse therapeutic effect may occur in that congestion may be stimulated rather than relieved.

The half-life of phenylephrine is about three hours. It takes fifteen hours from the last use of phenylephrine to its eventual clearance from the body.

Use of phenylephrine as a decongestant is permissible for a pilot providing prior approval is obtained from an AME. The condition for which it is used may preclude safe flight.

Generic name: *piperazine*
Brand names: *Antepar, Ascaril, Bryrel, Dayper, Multifuge, Multipar, Ogem, Oxy-Uriol, Panverm, Parazate, Perazine, Pin Tega, Pinrow, Piperazol, Pipercon, Pip-Zine, Piriflex, Rou-Medi-Pin, Tivazine, Verma-Hal, Vermitrate*
Usual dose: (varies)

Piperazine is used to treat intestinal infections by roundworms or pinworms.

In addition to its desired therapeutic effect, piperazine may cause adverse side effects. Examples of these side effects that are of significance to pilots include headache, spinning sensations, abdominal cramps, and nausea. Side effects, however, are usually mild and infrequent.

It is permissible to continue flight activities providing prior approval from an AME is obtained.

71

Generic name: *primaquin*
Usual dose: once weekly

Primaquin is an antimalarial drug. It is commonly used to protect people who enter an area where malaria exists.

In addition to its desired antimalarial effects, primaquin may cause unwanted side effects. Examples of these side effects that are of significance to pilots include nausea, blurred vision, difficulty in eye focusing, and impaired hearing.

With prior approval of an AME, flight activities may be continued while taking primaquin. If malaria is contracted or if side effects develop, suspend flying and consult an AME about future flight activities.

Generic name: *propoxyphene*
Brand names: *Barrigesic, Darvon, Dolaneed, Dolene, Myospaz Improved, Progesic, Propoxychel, Proxagesic, Proxene, S-Pain, Thera Von*
Usual dose: (varies)

Propoxyphene is used to relieve mild to moderate pain. Overuse may lead to addiction.

In addition to its desired therapeutic effects, propoxyphene may cause adverse side effects. Examples of these side effects that are of significance to pilots include diminished mental alertness, dizziness, headache, and weakness.

The half-life of propoxyphene is about four hours. It takes twenty hours from the time of the last dose to its eventual clearance from the body.

Use of propoxyphene while performing flight activities is permissible if prior approval is obtained from an AME. The condition causing the pain may preclude safe piloting duties.

Generic name: *pseudoephedrine*
Brand names: *Cenafed, Decofed, D-Feda, Neobid, Novafed, Pseudocot, Rynafed, Sudarine, Sufedrin*
Multi-ingredient drugs: Actacin, Actagen, Actamine, Actifed, Actilad, Acti-Med, Aerdil, Allefrin, Asmadil, Bronchobid, Corphed, Histafed, Pseudodine, Suda-Prol, Tagafed, Triacin, Triadrine, Triaphed, Trifed, Triposed, Triprolidine, Tri-Sudo, Trofedrine, Vantep
Usual dose: up to about 120 mg per day

Pseudoephedrine is used to treat congested nasal and other breathing passages. It can shrink nasal membranes and widen constricted breathing passageways.

In addition to its desired therapeutic effects, pseudoephedrine can cause adverse side effects. These side effects are usually mild and infrequent. Examples of side effects that are of significance to pilots include headache, dizziness, and restlessness.

The half-life of pseudoephedrine is about three hours. It takes fifteen hours from the last dose to the drug's eventual clearance from the body.

Flight duties may be continued while using pseudoephedrine, provided prior approval is obtained from an AME. It may be that the underlying problem precludes safe flight duties, treated or untreated. An AME can give advice in individual cases.

Generic name: *pyrimethamine*
Brand name: *Daraprim*
Usual dose: (varies)

Pyrimethamine is used to protect individuals from contracting malaria. It may also be used in the treatment of acute attacks of malaria. In much higher doses, pyrimethamine is used to treat acute toxoplasmosis.

In addition to its desired therapeutic effects, pyrimethamine may cause unwanted side effects. Examples of these side effects that are of interest to pilots include anemia, nausea, vomiting, and, infrequently, convulsions.

The half-life of pyrimethamine is about twelve hours. It takes two-and-one-half days from the last dose to the eventual clearance of the drug from the body.

With prior approval by an AME it is permissible to fly while using pyrimethamine for protection from malaria. If it is used to treat an acute attack of malaria or to treat toxoplasmosis, consult further with an AME. The disease may preclude safe pilot duties.

Generic name: *quinine*
Multi-ingredient drug: Quirea
Usual dose: 300–600 mg per day

Quinine is no longer a drug of choice for the treatment of malaria. It is used to treat certain kinds of nocturnal leg cramps.

In addition to its desired therapeutic effect, quinine may cause adverse side effects. Examples of these side effects that are of significance to pilots include "ringing" in the ears, dizziness, deafness, and visual disturbances.

Each user of quinine must be evaluated on an individual basis for continuation of flight activities with safety. Consult an AME about flight activities when quinine is prescribed. Quinine traces may linger in the body for days and even longer after its intake is discontinued. A few anecdotal reports indicate that the inner ear of some people may be affected adversely by quinine, leading to marked vertigo under instrument flight meteorological conditions. These reports have not been verified yet by research studies.

Generic name: *streptomycin*
Usual dose: 1–2 gm per day

Streptomycin is an antibiotic that is given only by injection, not by mouth. Over the course of the decades in which streptomycin has been used, many bacteria that were sensitive have developed resistance to this antibiotic. Many newer antibiotics are effective where streptomycin is not. For certain infections, however, streptomycin is still an excellent antibiotic. To minimize the likelihood that resistant bacteria will appear, streptomycin is commonly given together with another antibiotic.

A number of adverse side effects may affect those taking streptomycin. These include fever, nausea, vomiting, and loss of a sense of balance or equilibrium. Impaired hearing has also occurred.

The half-life of streptomycin is about six hours. Within two days of discontinuance, most of this drug will have been cleared from the body.

Consult an AME in regard to flying while taking streptomycin. The condition being treated may preclude safe flight.

Generic name: *sulfadiazine*

Multi-ingredient drugs: Chemozine, Cherasulfa, Lantrisul, Merabar, Neotrizine, Orbizine, Quadetts, Sulfalan, Sulfaloid, Sulfa Triple, Sulfazem, Sulfose, Terfonyl, Tersulfa, Three Sulfas, Tri Diazole, Trionamide, Triple Sulfa, Trisem, Trisulfa, Trisuval, Troisul

Usual dose: about 8 gm per day

Sulfadiazine is an antibacterial drug, a member of the sulfa drug group. It is given to treat infections by susceptible microbes. Often sulfadiazine is given in combination with one or two other sulfa drugs. In combination, the beneficial effects are additive, but the adverse side effects are often not.

In addition to the desired therapeutic effect, sulfadiazine may cause unwanted side effects. With one exception the side effects are usually mild and of little significance. The one side effect of note is the formation of crystals in the urinary tract. This is avoided by using sulfa drugs in combinations and by drinking adequate amounts of water to assure a plentiful urine flow.

It is permissible to continue flight activities while taking sulfadiazine if the condition for which it is taken does not preclude safe flight. The half-life of sulfadiazine is about six hours. It takes thirty hours from the last dose to the eventual clearance of the drug from the body.

Consult an AME if in doubt about pilot status when sulfadiazine has been prescribed.

Generic name: *sulfamethoxazole*

Brand names: *Gantanol, Methoxal, Microsul, Thiosulfil*

Multi-ingredient drugs: Azo Gantanol, Bactrim, Septra

Usual dose: 4 gm per day

Sulfamethoxazole is an antibacterial drug, a member of the sulfa drug group. It is used to treat infections caused by certain bacteria often found in the urinary tract.

In addition to the desired therapeutic effect, sulfamethoxazole may cause unwanted side effects. Examples of these side effects that are of significance to pilots include headache, skin rash, abdominal pains, and dizziness.

It is usually permissible to continue flight activities while taking sulfamethoxazole if the condition being treated is not too severe. The half-life of sulfamethoxazole is about eleven hours, and it takes two-and-one-half days from the last dose to the drug's essential clearance from the body.

If in doubt about the underlying condition's effect on pilot duties, consult an AME.

Generic name: *sulfisoxazole*
Brand names: *Barazole, Chemovag, Cheragan, Econo-Soxazole, Gantrex, Gantrisin, Jefazole, Niricin, Polysul, Rosoxol, SK-Soxazole, Sofrazol, Sosol, Soxitabs, Sulfagan, Sulfasox, Sul-Fed, Sulfisocon, Sulfizin, Sulfo-Hal, Sulsoxin, Truxazole, Urisoxin, Urozole, Zole-Lake*
Usual dose: 8–10 gm per day

Sulfisoxazole is an antibacterial drug, a member of the sulfa group. It is used to treat infections caused by suspectible microbes, especially those found in urinary tract infections.

In addition to its desired antibacterial effect, sulfisoxazole can cause unwanted side effects. Examples of these side effects that are of significance to pilots include pain in the abdomen, headache, and skin rash.

The half-life of sulfisoxazole is about five hours. It takes twenty-five hours to eventually clear the drug from the body following the last dose.

Consult an AME about flight duties while being treated with sulfisoxazole. A severe underlying infection will preclude safe flight duties. A treated asymptomatic, mild infection should present no problems, however, unless drug side effects are present.

Generic name: *sulindac*
Brand name: *Clinoril*
Usual dose: 400 mg per day

Sulindac is used to treat various kinds of arthritis, bursitis, and other joint discomforts.

In addition to its desired therapeutic effects, sulindac may cause unwanted side effects. Examples of these side effects that are of significance to pilots include diarrhea, skin rash, headache, and dizziness.

The half-life of sulindac is about sixteen hours. It takes three-and-one-half days from the last dose of sulindac to its eventual clearance from the body.

Consult an AME in regard to undertaking flight duties when sulindac has been prescribed. Each user of sulindac must be evaluated on an individual basis in regard to continued flight activities while taking the drug.

Generic name: *terbutaline*
Brand names: *Brethine, Bricanyl*
Usual dose: 15 mg per day

Terbutaline is used to ease breathing difficulty in asthma attacks. It helps to open constricted breathing passages.

In addition to its desired therapeutic effects, terbutaline can cause adverse side effects. Examples of these side effects that are of interest to pilots include nervousness, dizziness, headache, and muscle cramps.

Each user of terbutaline must be evaluated on an individual basis in relation to flight activities. Factors to be considered include both the impact of the terbutaline on the individual and the status of the asthma condition in regard to the safety of continued flight activities.

The half-life of terbutaline is about two hours. It takes ten hours from the time of the last dose to the drug's eventual clearance from the body.

When the asthma attack has passed and the terbutaline has been discontinued, consult an AME about future pilot duties.

Generic name: *thiphenamil*
Brand name: *Trocinate*
Usual dose: 800–1200 mg per day

Thiphenamil is used to treat irritable bowel syndrome of the large intestine. It is also used to treat stomach spasms.

In addition to its therapeutic effects, thiphenamil may cause unwanted side effects. Examples of these side effects that are of significance to pilots include drowsiness, blurred vision, constipation, or dry mouth.

Suspend flying when thiphenamil has been prescribed. Consult an AME on flight duties. The condition being treated or the side effects of the drug may preclude safe flight.

Generic name: *tolmetin*
Brand name: *Tolectin*
Usual dose: (varies)

Tolmetin is used in the treatment of various kinds of arthritis.

In addition to its desired therapeutic effect, tolmetin can cause adverse side effects. Examples of these side effects that are of significance to

77

pilots include nausea, abdominal pain, headache, nervousness, and drowsiness.

Each user of tolmetin must be evaluated on an individual basis for capability to continue flight activities with safety. When tolmetin is prescribed, consult an AME or the FAA in regard to flight duties. The severity of the condition treated and the presence of side effects will determine flight status when under treatment.

It takes two days from the last dose to eventually clear the drug from the body.

Generic name: *trimethoprim*
Brand names: *Proloprim, Trimpex*
Multi-ingredient drugs: Bactrim, Septra
Usual dose: 200 mg per day

Trimethoprim is an antibacterial drug. It is used in the treatment of infections, commonly in the urinary tract.

In addition to its desired antibacterial effect, trimethoprim can cause unwanted side effects. Examples of these side reactions that are of significance to pilots include skin rash, fever, nausea, and vomiting.

The half-life of trimethoprim is about ten hours. It takes fifty hours from the time of the last dose to eventually clear the drug from the body.

If the infection is mild and there are no side effects from the drug, pilot duties may be continued while taking trimethoprim. If in doubt, consult an AME.

Generic name: *vancomycin*
Brand name: *Vancocin*
Usual dose: 2 gm per day

Vancomycin is an antibiotic used to treat infections caused by certain bacteria. Vancomycin is not a commonly used antibiotic, like penicillin. It is beneficial, however, when the infecting bacteria are sensitive to vancomycin.

Adverse side effects can occur, including nausea, chills, or fever. Check with an AME prior to flying as a pilot when under treatment with vancomycin. The condition being treated may preclude safe performance as a pilot.

The half-life of vancomycin is estimated to be about six hours. If flying is suspended, allow one day between the last dose and the resumption of flying.

Chapter 7

Category III Drugs: Flight Duties Are Approved in Individual Cases

Drugs in this category will generally preclude safe piloting, although the FAA may approve flight activities in individual cases. Refer to the individual drug listings here for more specific information about a drug's effects on flight activities.

As always, consult an AME or the FAA if any question remains about the advisability of flying while taking one of these drugs.

Generic name: *acetazolamide*
Brand name: *Diamox*
Usual dose: 1–1.5 gm per day

Acetazolamide is used to help remove excess fluid that has accumulated in the tissues and to treat certain kinds of glaucoma.

The half-life of acetazolamide is about six hours. Twenty-four hours following discontinuation of the drug most of it will have cleared from the body.

The intended medicinal effect of acetazolamide may be accompanied by undesired side effects. Side effects of interest to pilots include drowsiness and confusion. It may also cause kidney stones. The safety of pilot duties while taking acetazolamide must be evaluated on an individual basis. Consult the FAA in regard to piloting while taking Diamox; the condition for which it is taken may preclude safe pilot duties.

Generic name: *allopurinol*
Brand names: *Lopurin, Zyloprim*
Usual dose: 200–800 mg per day

Allopurinol is used in the treatment of gout. It is used to prevent the formation of uric acid deposits in the various susceptible parts of the body, including the joints. It functions to reduce the production of uric acid.

In addition to the desired therapeutic effects, allopurinol may cause adverse side effects, some of which are mild and others quite severe. Examples of side effects of interest to pilots include skin rash, nausea, vomiting, and diarrhea.

The half-life of allopurinol is about three hours. One day after drug discontinuation will see clearance of most of the drug from the body.

Consult the FAA concerning pilot duties while taking allopurinol. Each pilot is assessed individually in regard to the safety of pilot duties. FAA approval is required.

Generic name: *aminosalicylic acid*
Brand names: *Parasal, P.A.S., Rezipas, Teebacin acid*
Multi-ingredient drugs: Di-Isopacin, Neo Hal Pas, Neopasalate, Neo-Teebacin acid, Parasal-INH
Usual dose: 10–12 gm per day

Aminosalicylic acid is used as a component in certain treatments of tuberculosis along with other antituberculosis drugs.

In addition to its beneficial therapeutic effects, however, aminosalicylic acid may cause adverse side effects. Examples of these side effects that are of significance to pilots include abdominal pain, diarrhea, nausea, and vomiting. Skin rash may also occur.

The half-life of aminosalicylic acid is one hour. After five hours, the body is almost totally cleared of the drug.

The FAA must be consulted prior to undertaking pilot duties while on this drug. The condition for which the drug is taken may preclude safe flight activities.

Generic name: *benzdroflumethiazide*
Brand name: *Naturetin*
Multi-ingredient drugs: Rautrax, Rauzide
Usual dose: 2.5–15 mg per day

Benzdroflumethiazide is used to rid the body of excess fluid that may collect in the tissues under certain conditions. Also, benzdroflumethiazide acts to reduce high blood pressure. It is often effective by itself in controlling high blood pressure. When it is not sufficient by itself, it can be used along with another blood-pressure-reducing drug. Two drugs used together sometimes provide an effect on high blood pressure greater than the sum of the effect of each drug.

Along with its intended medicinal effects, benzdroflumethiazide may cause adverse side reactions. These side reactions may affect the stomach, the remaining digestive tract, the blood, the circulatory system, the nervous system, and other systems.

Some of the side effects of interest to pilots are nausea, vomiting, stomach pain, diarrhea, dizziness, and weakness, to cite just a few. Consult the FAA prior to flying while on this drug. Piloting while taking benzdroflumethiazide for high blood pressure may be approved on an individual basis. If the control of high blood pressure requires another drug along with benzdroflumethiazide, piloting may not be permitted. The second drug may cause a decrease in G tolerance that would be hazardous to pilots.

The half-life of this drug is estimated to be about six hours. Allow two days to clear the drug from the body.

Generic name: *benzthiazide*
Brand names: *Amuret, Aqua-Fed, Aquamast, Aquapres, Aquex, Benzide, Diuride, Edemex, Exna, Hydrex, Marazide, Omuretic, Urazide*
Multi-ingredient drug: Exna-R
Usual dose: 50–200 mg per day

Benzthiazide is used to clear excess fluids that collect in the body and to reduce high blood pressure. For high blood pressure, benzthiazide may be used alone or with other kinds of drugs that reduce blood pressure.

Like other prescription drugs, the intended medicinal effect may carry with it unwanted side effects. These can affect the digestive tract, the circulating blood, the skin, and other parts of the body. Upon arising abruptly from a reclining position, a person taking this drug may feel lightheaded or dizzy. Side effects that may interfere with flying include weakness (from potassium loss), stomach discomfort, nausea, vomiting, skin rash, headache, or feelings of dizziness.

If benzthiazide is being taken alone, flight duties may be approved by the FAA. If there is significant pathology present (for example, kidney disease), approval may not be given.

The half-life of benzthiazide is short, about three hours.

Generic name: *capreomycin*
Brand name: *Capastat*
Usual dose: 1 gm per day

Capreomycin is an antibiotic that is effective against organisms that cause tuberculosis. It is usually one of two or more drugs used together in the treatment program.

Capreomycin is a potent drug, which may have powerful adverse side effects. Loss of hearing may accompany use of capreomycin. In most instances, hearing returns to normal after use of capreomycin ends.

Each person taking capreomycin should be evaluated on an individual basis in regard to continuing flight duties. Consult an AME for a decision in this regard. The decision will depend on the underlying infectious condition, the state of general health, and manifest side effects of the medicines taken. The response of the condition to treatment will also be considered.

Generic name: *chlorothiazide*
Brand names: *Chlorulan, Diurigen, Diuril*
Multi-ingredient drugs: Aldoclor, Chloroserp, Chloroserpine, Diupres, Theda C-Res, Thiaserp
Usual dose: .5–1 gm per day

Chlorothiazide is a popular drug used to remove excess fluid that may accumulate in the tissues and to bring high blood pressure down toward normal. Chlorothiazide may be used alone or with other drugs that also reduce high blood pressure.

In addition to its medicinal actions, chlorothiazide may cause one or more side reactions. These side reactions can affect many parts of the body, including the digestive tract, the blood and its circulation, and the skin.

Chlorothiazide has a half-life of about two hours. This means that within a day after stopping chlorothiazide, the drug is mostly cleared from the body.

If the FAA gives approval, piloting is permissible while taking chlorothiazide. If chlorothiazide is being used in combination with another blood-pressure-reducing drug, a new approval must be obtained.

Generic name: *chlorthalidone*
Brand name: *Hygroton*
Multi-ingredient drugs: Combipres, Regroton
Usual dose: 25–100 mg per day

Chlorthalidone is used to aid in controlling high blood pressure. It may be used alone or together with another blood-pressure-reducing drug. The advantage that may be gained using two drugs is that the desired effect on the blood pressure may be achieved with lower doses of the two drugs than with a higher dose of either one used alone. Because the degree of adverse side effects is often proportional to the dose given, lower doses of two drugs are usually safer than a higher dose of a single drug.

The side effects of chlorthalidone may provoke symptoms from the stomach and digestive system, the nervous system, the heart, and other parts of the body. Adverse effects of interest to pilots include diarrhea, nausea, vomiting, feelings of dizziness upon standing, and generalized weakness.

The half-life of chlorthalidone is about seventy-two hours. Clearance of chlorthalidone from the body to negligible levels requires at least nine days.

Flying while taking chlorthalidone is permissible if the FAA approves.

Generic name: *cimetidine*
Brand name: *Tagamet*
Usual dose: 1200 mg per day

Cimetidine acts to reduce the amount of acid secreted into the stomach. It is used for relief of peptic ulcers and other conditions that are aggravated by the secretion of too much acid into the stomach.

In addition to the desired medicinal effects, cimetidine may cause adverse side effects. Examples of these adverse side effects that are of significance to pilots include muscular pain, diarrhea, and dizziness.

The half-life of cimetidine is two hours. By one day following the last dose virtually all of the drug is gone from the body.

Consult with the FAA before undertaking pilot duties when taking cimetidine. The condition for which it is taken may preclude safe flight.

Generic name: *clofibrate*
Brand name: *Atromid-S*
Usual dose: up to 2 gm per day

Clofibrate is used to lower the level of cholesterol in the blood. It may also assist in reducing the levels of other fats in the blood.

In addition to its desired medicinal effects, clofibrate may cause a variety of side effects. These adverse side effects may appear in many different ways. Examples of adverse side effects of interest to pilots are nausea, muscle cramps, drowsiness, and headache. It has been reported also that gallstones may form in some persons as a result of taking this drug.

The half-life of clofibrate is about twelve hours. It should be mentioned that a major airline has in the past placed large numbers of their pilots on clofibrate with no reported difficulties.

Whether or not it is safe to fly while using clofibrate needs to be determined on an individual basis. Consult with the FAA prior to flying when planning to use clofibrate.

Generic name: *colchicine*
Multi-ingredient drugs: Acetycol, Bricolide, Colbenemid, Colsalide, Nugen, Salcolc, Salisicol, S-P-C
Usual dose: (varies)

Colchicine is used to treat gout. It works in part to prevent the accumulation of uric acid in joint spaces and tendon sheaths. It may interrupt acute attacks of gouty arthritis by inhibiting neutrophil migration into the areas where uric acid may be depositing.

To be really effective, colchicine must be used early, prior to the full development of an attack of gout. Sometimes the effective dose for relief may approach a level that can cause adverse side effects. These adverse side effects may include nausea, vomiting, diarrhea, and suppression of white blood cell production.

The question of the safety of continued flight activity while taking colchicine must be decided on an individual basis. The FAA must be consulted for approval to fly while taking colchicine.

The half-life of colchicine is about six hours. If flying is suspended, allow two days between the last dose and the resumption of flying.

Generic name: *cromolyn*
Brand name: *Intal*
Usual dose: (varies)

Cromolyn is used to treat bronchial asthma. It is taken either with an inhaler or by mouth in capsules.

In addition to its desired medicinal effects, cromolyn may cause certain unwanted side effects. Although a variety of side effects may be seen, the most common adverse effects are on the respiratory system. These include coughing, wheezing, throat irritation, or stuffy nose.

Each user of cromolyn has to be assessed individually with regard to the safety of continued flying. Consult the FAA for approval to fly while using cromolyn. The asthmatic condition for which the cromolyn is taken may preclude safe pilot duties.

Generic name: *cycloserine*
Brand name: *Seromycin*
Usual dose: .5–1 gm per day

Cycloserine is an antibiotic drug used in the treatment of tuberculosis. It is used in conjunction with another antituberculosis drug. Infrequently, cycloserine may be used to treat urinary tract infections.

In addition to its intended medicinal effect, cycloserine may cause adverse side effects. Examples of side effects of interest to fliers are headache, dizziness, and confusion.

The half-life of cycloserine is about two hours. Within one day following discontinuation virtually all of the drug should be cleared from the body.

Consult the FAA concerning flight duties while taking cycloserine. The condition being treated may preclude safe flight.

Generic name: *cyclothiazide*
Brand name: *Anhydron*
Usual dose: 2–6 mg per day

Cyclothiazide is used to help relieve the accumulation of body fluids associated with many kinds of illness. It also may reduce high blood pressure.

A variety of side effects can occur, including excess losses of potassium, sodium, or chloride from the blood. Other side effects that may occur include "sour" stomach, nausea, vomiting, and dizziness.

The half-life of cyclothiazide is about two hours.

With FAA approval, pilot duties may be approved while taking cyclothiazide. If cyclothiazide is being taken together with one or more other drugs, flying ability may be impaired through drug interaction.

Generic name: *dextrothyroxin*
Brand name: *Choloxin*
Usual dose: 4–8 mg per day

Dextrothyroxin is used to reduce the level of cholesterol in the blood and to make up for an underfunctioning thyroid gland.

In addition to the desired medicinal effects, dextrothyroxin may cause a variety of adverse side effects. Examples of side effects that are of interest to pilots are various heart changes, sweating, increased production of urine, menstrual irregularities, nausea, and dizziness.

Safety of flight activities while taking dextrothyroxin depends on many factors, such as the general condition of the individual, the effects of the dextrothyroxin, and the condition being treated. Consult the FAA prior to flying as a pilot while under treatment with Choloxin.

Generic name: *epinephrine*
Brand names: *Adrenalin, Asmolin, Epinal, Eppy N, Sus-Phrine*
Usual dose: (varies)

Epinephrine is a potent drug with a variety of uses. Injected, it may be used to open blocked or constricted breathing passages. These may occur in asthma attacks or in certain kinds of allergic reactions. When inhaled, it may provide relief from an attack of difficult breathing due to asthma. It is also used to treat certain types of "chronic simple" or "wide-angle" glaucoma.

Along with its desired effects epinephrine may cause adverse side effects. Examples of these effects that are of interest to pilots are headache, rapid heart rate, and acutely elevated blood pressure.

Generally, flight duties should not be continued while using epinephrine. The condition for which the epinephrine is prescribed may constitute a hazard to safe pilot duties. FAA approval is necessary prior to flight while taking epinephrine.

Generic name: *ethacrynic acid*
Brand name: *Edecrin*
Usual dose: 50–200 mg per day

Ethacrynic acid is used to increase the production of urine in the body. It is a more powerful drug than many others for the removal of excess tissue fluids.

Along with promoting the removal of fluids ethacrynic acid may cause changes in the amounts of certain substances in the blood, such as sodium, potassium, or chloride. Blood tests can alert the physician to changes that may be significant. Usually the body regulates the amounts of these substances in the blood within close limits.

In addition to its intended medicinal effect, ethacrynic acid may also cause adverse side reactions of significance to pilots. Hearing may be affected and dizziness may be felt. Other side reactions include nausea, vomiting, diarrhea, difficulty in swallowing, and headache.

The half-life of ethacrynic acid is about six hours. Two days after the last dose will allow most of the ethacrynic acid to be cleared from the body.

Flying may be permitted when taking ethacrynic acid provided that the FAA gives individual approval. The condition under treatment, however, may preclude safe flight.

Generic name: *ethambutol*
Brand name: *Myambutol*
Usual dose: (depends on weight)

Ethambutol is used to treat tuberculosis. It is most effective when used with other antituberculosis drugs.

Along with its intended therapeutic effect, ethambutol may cause adverse side effects. The principal side effect of great interest to pilots is impaired vision. Other side effects are fever, headache, nausea, vomiting, and dizziness.

The half-life of ethambutol is about eight hours. Two days following discontinuation should see almost full clearance of the drug from the body.

Consult the FAA in regard to pilot duties while taking ethambutol. The condition being treated may preclude safe flight.

Generic name: *furosemide*
Brand name: *Lasix*
Usual dose: 20–80 mg per day

Furosemide is used to remove the excess fluids that collect in the tissues of the body in certain illnesses. Furosemide may also be effective in controlling high blood pressure. For the treatment of high blood pressure furosemide can be used alone or together with another blood-pressure-reducing drug.

In addition to the desired medicinal effect, adverse side reactions may occur. These side reactions are not common, but they may be of significance when they arise. Certain side effects may arise if the amounts of salts in the blood change excessively. As a result, the individual may feel weak or drowsy.

Other significant adverse reactions that may affect the stomach and remaining digestive tract, the blood, and other parts of the body include headache, nausea, vomiting, blurred vision, diarrhea, and skin rash.

The half-life of furosemide is about six hours. Allow one day following the last dose of furosemide for essential clearance of the drug from the body.

Consult the FAA for approval to fly while taking this medication. Decisions are based on individual considerations.

Generic name: *griseofulvin*
Brand names: *Fulvicin, Grifulvin, Grisactin, Grisowen, Gris-Peg*
Usual dose: 500 mg per day

Griseofulvin is an antibiotic that is effective against certain kinds of fungi, including many different kinds of ringworm.

In addition to its desired medicinal effects, griseofulvin may give rise to adverse side effects. Examples of these side effects that are of significance to fliers include skin rash, hives, nausea, vomiting, or dizziness.

The half-life of griseofulvin is about twelve hours. Two days following treatment cessation, most of the drug should be cleared from the body.

Consult with the FAA in regard to flight duties when taking griseofulvin.

Generic name: *hydrochlorothiazide*
Brand names: *Amuret-H, Aqua-Hal, Aquamet, Carozide, Diucen-H, Diuretin, Dydro-D, Esidrix, Hydrochlor, Hydrochlorulan, Hydroeze, Hydrokraft, Hydromal, Hydrotab, Hydro-Z, Hydrozide-Z, Mictrin, Oretic, Randuril, Tenzide, Thianal, Thiuretic, X-Aqua*
Multi-ingredient drugs: Aldactazide, Aldoril, Apresazide, Butizide, Caparil, Dyazide, Esimil, Hydropres, Hydroserp, Hydroserpine, Hydrotensin, Inderide, Mallopres, Oreticyl, Ser-Ap-Es, Sterapres, Thianal-R, Thiopres, Unipres
Usual dose: 50–100 mg per day

Hydrochlorothiazide is used to remove fluid that collects in the tissues under certain conditions. It is also used to control high blood pressure. For treatment of high blood pressure, hydrochlorothiazide may be used alone or, on occasion, with another blood-pressure-reducing drug. In this latter instance, each drug may enhance the effect of the other.

In addition to its intended medicinal effect, hydrochlorothiazide may cause side effects. The reported side effects are numerous and varied, but they occur in only a small fraction of people who take hydrochlorothiazide. Side effects of significance to pilots include diarrhea, nausea, vomiting, dizziness, and headaches.

The half-life is about four hours. One day following drug cessation should see clearance of most of the drug from the body.

Use of hydrochlorothiazide may be approved by the FAA in individual cases. If used in combination with certain other drugs, pilot duties may not be approved.

Generic name: *hydroflumethiazide*
Brand names: *Diucardin, Saluron*
Multi-ingredient drug: Salutensin
Usual doses: (varies)

Hydroflumethiazide is used to treat the accumulation of excess fluids in the tissues and to help reduce high blood pressure toward normal levels. In treating high blood pressure, hydroflumethiazide may be used alone or with other blood-pressure-reducing drugs.

In addition to its desired beneficial effects, hydroflumethiazide may cause adverse side effects. Examples of these side effects that may be of significance to pilots include dizzy or lightheaded feelings (especially shortly after standing from a reclining position) and headaches.

The effect of hydroflumethiazide upon piloting ability must be individually evaluated. Consult with an AME in regard to approval for pilot duties while taking hydroflumethiazide.

Generic name: *isoetharine*
Brand name: *Bronkosol*
Usual dose: (used in the form of a spray)

Isoetharine is used to relieve the breathing difficulties accompanying bronchial asthma. It helps to open constricted breathing passages.

In addition to its desired therapeutic effect isoetharine can cause adverse side effects. Examples of these side effects that are of interest to pilots include nausea, headache, anxiety, and restlessness.

Each user of isoetharine must be evaluated on an individual basis for capability to continue flight activities with safety. Consult an AME or the FAA in regard to future flight activities when isoetharine has been prescribed.

Generic name: *isoniazid*
Brand names: *INH, Isohydrazide, Isonicotinic acid hydrazide, Laniazid, Nicozide, Nydrazid, Teebaconin*
Multi-ingredient drugs: Panazide BG, P-I-N Forte, Rifamate, Rimactane, Rimactazid
Usual dose: 300 mg per day

Isoniazid is used in the treatment of tuberculosis. It may be used in combination with other drugs.

As with other drugs, isoniazid may cause certain side effects that may adversely affect performance of flight duties. Examples of side effects of interest to pilots include skin reactions, nausea, and vomiting.

The half-life of isoniazid is about eight hours. Two days after the last dose should see essentially full clearance of the drug from the body.

Consult the FAA in regard to flying while taking isoniazid. The condition for which the drug is being taken may preclude safe flight.

Generic name: *liothyronine*
Synonym: *triiodothyronine*
Brand name: *Cytomel*
Usual dose: (varies)

Liothyronine is used to treat insufficient thyroid hormone production and to treat certain kinds of goiter.

In addition to its intended therapeutic effects, liothyronine may cause unwanted side effects. Examples of adverse effects that are of significance to pilots include nervousness, headache, irregularities in heartbeat, and sweating.

The half-life of liothyronine is about two-and-one-half hours. The actions of the medication, however, may continue for days, even weeks, following cessation of intake.

Each user of liothyronine must be evaluated on an individual basis for continuation of flight activities. Consult with the FAA when liothyronine is prescribed. The condition for which it is given may preclude safe flight.

Generic name: *liotrix*
Brand names: *Euthroid, Thyrolar*
Usual dose: (varies)

Liotrix is a thyroid hormone preparation that is used to treat conditions arising from inadequate amounts of thyroid hormone produced by the thyroid gland.

In addition to its desired medicinal effects, liotrix may cause adverse effects that may be eliminated by reducing the dose of liotrix. Examples of these adverse effects of significance to pilots include menstrual irregularities, nervousness, headache, and sweating.

Consult the FAA prior to conducting pilot duties when liotrix is prescribed. The condition for which the drug is taken may preclude safe flight.

Generic name: *mecamylamine*
Brand name: *Inversine*
Usual dose: (varies)

Mecamylamine is used in the treatment of moderate to severe high blood pressure. It is generally not used for mild high blood pressure, but rather is reserved for cases that do not respond to other drugs. Often it is used in combination with other blood-pressure-reducing drugs.

In addition to its desired therapeutic effect, mecamylamine can cause unwanted side effects. Examples of these side effects that are of significance to pilots include diarrhea, dry mouth, blurred vision, and mental aberrations.

The half-life of mecamylamine is estimated to be about twenty-four hours. It takes five days to clear the drug from the body following the last dose.

Each user of mecamylamine must be evaluated on an individual basis for capability to continue flight activities. Consult an AME or the FAA when mecamylamine has been prescribed.

Generic name: *methyclothiazide*
Brand names: *Aquatensen, Enduron*
Multi-ingredient drugs: Diutensen, Enduronyl, Eutron
Usual dose: 2.5–5 mg per day

Methyclothiazide is used to remove excess fluid from the body's tissues and to bring high blood pressure levels back toward normal. Attempted control of blood pressure is the most common use of this drug. Methyclothiazide can be given by itself or with other blood-pressure-reducing drugs.

A variety of side effects occur along with desired medicinal effects. Most important are symptoms of weakness, drowsiness, or muscle pains that may arise from excessive loss of potassium or other salts. Other side reactions may be nausea, vomiting, skin rash, or hives. A dizzy or lightheaded feeling may result from abruptly standing after lying down.

The half-life of methyclothiazide is short, about two hours.

Flying is permissible while taking methyclothiazide if the FAA gives approval. Each case is decided individually. If the drug is being used with another blood-pressure-reducing drug, flying ability may be impaired and flight approval may not be granted.

Generic name: *naproxen*
Brand names: *Anaprox, Naprosyn*
Usual dose: (varies)

Naproxen is used in the treatment of rheumatoid arthritis and osteo-arthritis. It is also used to relieve pain and for relief of painful menstruation.

In addition to its desired therapeutic effects, naproxen may cause unwanted side effects. Examples of these side effects that are of interest to pilots include dizziness, drowsiness, heartburn, and headache.

The half-life of naproxen is about thirteen hours. It takes three days following the last dose for an essential clearance of the drug from the body.

Each user of naproxen must be evaluated on an individual basis for determination of ability to continue flight activities with safety. Consult an AME or the FAA when naproxen is prescribed. The conditions for which it is prescribed may preclude safe flight duties, as may the side effects experienced in individual cases.

Generic name: *pargyline*
Brand name: *Eutonyl*
Usual dose: (varies)

Pargyline is used in the treatment of high blood pressure. Often it is used in combination with other blood-pressure-reducing drugs.

In addition to its desired therapeutic effect, pargyline may cause adverse side effects. Examples of these side effects that are of significance to pilots include dizziness, weakness, hallucinations, and blurred vision.

The half-life of pargyline is about six hours. It takes about thirty hours from the time of the last dose to pargyline's eventual clearance from the body.

Each pilot using pargyline must be evaluated on an individual basis by the FAA to determine if flight activities may be continued with safety.

Generic name: *phenylbutazone*
Brand names: *Azolid, Butazolidin*
Multi-ingredient drug: Butazolidin Alka
Usual dose: (varies)

Phenylbutazone is a nonsteroid that has a variety of uses. It is used to achieve symptomatic relief from certain arthritic conditions including gouty arthritis, rheumatoid arthritis, and ankylosing spondylitis. It may be used for relief of pain in certain diseases of various joints such as the hips, knees, or shoulders. It also reduces fever.

In addition to its desired therapeutic effects, phenylbutazone may cause adverse side effects. Examples of these side effects that are of significance to pilots include abdominal distress, headache, drowsiness, and weakness.

The half-life of phenylbutazone is about one hundred hours. It takes thirteen days from the last dose to the time of eventual clearance of the drug from the body.

When phenylbutazone is prescribed, consult the FAA. Each user of phenylbutazone must be evaluated individually in regard to future flight activities. Factors that are to be considered include the nature and severity of the condition being treated plus the response to phenylbutazone.

93

Generic name: *polythiazide*
Brand name: *Renese*
Multi-ingredient drugs: Minizide, Renese-R
Usual dose: 2–4 mg per day

Polythiazide is used to clear excess fluid that accumulates in the tissues in certain illnesses and to reduce blood pressure when it is higher than normal. This drug can be used as the sole means of controlling high blood pressure or it can be used with another drug. When used with another drug, the blood-pressure-reducing effects may be enhanced and adverse reactions lessened.

Among the adverse side effects are those that can affect the stomach and remaining digestive tract, nervous tissue, circulatory system, skin, and other parts of the body. Examples of side effects include stomach irritation, nausea, vomiting, deafness, headache, weakness, and skin rash.

The half-life of polythiazide is about two hours. Within one day following discontinuation, most of the drug is gone from the body.

Use of polythiazide is compatible with safe piloting if approved by the FAA. When polythiazide is one of a combination of drugs being taken, flying may not be approved because of adverse side effects of the second drug.

Generic name: *prazosin*
Brand name: *Minipress*
Usual dose: (varies)

Prazosin is used to bring high blood pressure down toward normal levels. It may be used alone or in combination with other blood-pressure-reducing drugs.

In addition to its desired therapeutic effects, prazosin may cause adverse side effects. Examples of these adverse side effects that are of significance to pilots include dizziness, headache, drowsiness, and weakness.

The half-life of prazosin is about three hours. It takes fifteen hours for the drug to clear the body following discontinuation of use.

Each user of prazosin must be evaluated on an individual basis in regard to continued pilot duties while taking prazosin. Consult the FAA when prazosin is prescribed. The drug may be a hazard if it decreases a pilot's tolerance to inflight G forces.

Generic name: *probenecid*
Brand names: *Benacen, Benemid, Probalan, Proben*
Multi-ingredient drugs: Colbenemid, Polycillin-PRB
Usual dose: 1 gm per day

Probenecid is used in the treatment of gout and to enhance the effects of certain antibiotics and other drugs. Probenecid works to promote the loss of uric acid through the urine.

Along with its intended beneficial effects, probenecid produces adverse side effects. Some adverse effects of interest to pilots include headache, nausea, vomiting, and dizziness.

Probenecid has a half-life of about twelve hours. Two days after discontinuation of the drug most of it will be cleared from the body.

Consult the FAA in regard to flight duties while taking probenecid. The condition being treated may preclude safe flight.

Generic name: *propantheline*
Brand names: *Amthine, Gastrical, Giquel, Mast-Bid, Norpanth, Panthene, Probanthine, Robantaline, Ropanth*
Usual dose: 75 mg per day

Propantheline is used to assist in the treatment of peptic ulcers.

In addition to its desired therapeutic effect, propantheline may cause certain adverse side effects. Examples of these side effects that are of significance to pilots are drowsiness, blurred vision, weakness, and mental confusion.

The half-life of propantheline is about four hours. It takes twenty hours between the last dose and the drug's eventual clearance from the body.

Continued flight duties of each user of propantheline must be evaluated on an individual basis. When propantheline is prescribed, consult the FAA in regard to flight activities. The underlying peptic ulcer problems may preclude safe flight, treated or untreated.

Generic name: *propranolol*
Brand name: *Inderal*
Multi-ingredient drug: Inderide
Usual dose: 40–480 mg per day (high blood pressure)

Propranolol is used to control high blood pressure, either alone or with another blood-pressure-reducing drug. It may be used for other heart disease problems, including abnormal heart rhythms. It also has been used to prevent migraine headaches.

In addition to its intended medicinal effect, propranolol may cause adverse reactions. These side reactions can vary widely. Side reactions can affect the heart, the nervous system, the stomach and remaining digestive tract, and other parts of the body. Examples of possible adverse effects of significance to pilots include lightheadedness, weakness, fatigue, nausea, and vomiting.

The half-life of propranolol is about three hours. One day after the last dose, the body is essentially cleared of the drug.

Since propranolol is used for some conditions that are themselves disqualifying, the FAA must be consulted in regard to approval for pilot duties. Approval is given depending on individual circumstances.

Generic name: *propylthiouracil*
Brand name: *Propacil*
Usual dose: 100–150 mg per day

Propylthiouracil is used to treat excessive activity of the thyroid gland. It decreases the amount of thyroid hormones produced by the gland and subsequently put into the circulating blood.

In addition to its desired therapeutic effect, propylthiouracil may cause adverse side effects. Examples of these side effects that are of significance to pilots include headache, drowsiness, dizziness, and fever.

The half-life of propylthiouracil is about eighteen hours. It takes fifty-four hours from the last dose for the drug to clear from the body.

Continued flight duties of users of propylthiouracil must be evaluated individually. When use of propylthiouracil begins, consult with the FAA about continued flight activities.

The determination of future flight duties will rest in part on the status of the underlying hyperthyroid activity, its cause, its effects on the body, and the effectiveness of the treatment in returning the individual's symptoms toward normal.

Generic name: *rifampin*
Brand names: *Rifadin, Rimactane*
Multi-ingredient drug: Rifamate
Usual dose: 600 mg per day

Rifampin is an antibiotic with limited uses. It is used in preventive treatment and, when used with other drugs, it is effective in the treatment of tuberculosis.

Rifampin may cause adverse side effects. Adverse reactions affecting pilots include heartburn, pain in the upper abdomen, nausea, vomiting, gas, cramps, drowsiness, and skin rash.

The half-life of rifampin is five hours. Within two days most of the drug will be cleared from the body.

The safety of piloting while taking rifampin must be considered on an individual basis. The condition for which the antibiotic is taken (the clinical status of the tuberculosis under treatment, for example) may preclude safe flight duties.

Generic name: *spironolactone*
Brand name: *Aldactone*
Multi-ingredient drug: Aldactazide
Usual dose: 100 mg per day

Spironolactone is used in connection with certain hormone therapy to relieve accumulation of excess fluids in the tissues. It is also used as an aid in controlling high blood pressure. Often, spironolactone is used together with another drug to reduce blood pressure. Spironolactone causes sodium and water to be excreted.

In addition to its medicinal effects spironolactone may cause adverse side effects. In some instances, significant changes in the amounts of sodium and chloride in the blood can result from the drug's use. This can lead to side effects of weakness and drowsiness. Other possible side effects of significance to pilots are diarrhea, headache, and mental confusion.

The half-life of spironolactone is estimated as twenty-four hours. Within three days following discontinuation of the drug most will be cleared from the body.

Consult the FAA about pilot duties when under treatment with spironolactone. Decisions are made on an individual basis.

Generic name: *sulfinpyrazone*
Brand name: *Anturane*
Usual dose: 400 mg per day

Sulfinpyrazone is used in the treatment of chronic or intermittent gout.

In addition to its desired therapeutic effect, sulfinpyrazone may cause adverse side effects. Examples of these side effects that are of significance to pilots include skin rash, upset stomach, and rarely, nausea.

The half-life of sulfinpyrazone is about twenty-four hours. It takes five days following the last dose to clear the body of the drug.

Continued flight duties of users of sulfinpyrazone should be evaluated on an individual basis by the FAA. The effectiveness of sulfinpyrazone in controlling the gout will be a major consideration.

Generic name: *thyroglobulin*
Brand name: *Proloid*
Usual dose: (varies)

Thyroglobulin is used to replace thyroid hormone or supplement inadequate levels of thyroid hormone production. It may be used to treat certain kinds of goiter (enlarged thyroid).

In addition to its desired hormone replacement effects, thyroglobulin can cause adverse side effects. Examples of these side effects that are of significance to pilots include menstrual irregularities, nervousness, and abnormal heart rhythms.

Continued flight duties of users of thyroglobulin must be evaluated on an individual basis. Consult the FAA in regard to future flight duties when thyroglobulin has been prescribed.

Generic name: *thyroid extract*
Brand names: *Deporoid, Omaloids, Parloid, Porkee, Thermoloid, Thyrar, Thyrocaps, Thyrocrine, Thyrodine, Thytropar*
Usual dose: (varies)

Thyroid extract is used to treat diminished thyroid function. Inadequate thyroid function may cause a variety of changes, including thickened skin, lowered metabolism, gain in weight, and heart failure.

In addition to its desired hormone replacement effects, thyroid can cause adverse side effects. Usually these side effects are no more serious than a mild stomach upset. Each user of thyroid extract, however, must have a carefully adjusted dose. If an excessive amount is taken over time nervousness, sweating, high heart rate, weight loss, and elevated body temperature can occur.

The half-life of thyroid is about seven days. It takes five weeks following the last dose to clear the drug from the body.

Continued flight duties of users of thyroid must be evaluated individually. Consult the FAA in regard to flight duties when thyroid extract has been prescribed.

Generic name: *thyroxine*
Synonyms: *L-thyroxine, sodium levothyroxine*
Brand name: *Synthroid*
Usual dose: (varies)

Thyroxine is a hormone produced by the thyroid gland. It is used to treat thyroid gland deficiency that arises from a nonfunctioning or underfunctioning thyroid gland. It may be used alone or with other thyroid hormones.

In addition to its desired hormone replacement effects, thyroxine may give adverse effects. Usually these are no more serious than an upset stomach. Other side effects may occur including nervousness, diarrhea, abnormal heart rhythm, and weight loss.

Consult the FAA when thyroxine use is required. Individual assessments are made concerning future flight duties.

Generic name: *triamterene*
Brand name: *Dyrenium*
Multi-ingredient drug: Dyazide
Usual dose: 100–200 mg per day

Triamterene is used to remove excess fluid that accumulates in the tissues in certain illnesses. Along with its medicinal fluid-clearing effect, triamterene may cause changes in the normal levels of certain salts in the circulating blood.

Varied adverse side effects may occur. Effects of significance to pilots include weakness, headache, nausea, and vomiting.

Triamterene has a half-life of about eighteen hours. Three days after discontinuation of use most of the drug will be cleared from the body.

Consult the FAA concerning piloting duties while on triamterene. The condition under treatment may preclude safe flight.

Generic name: *trichlormethiazide*
Brand names: *Aquazide, Diurese, Metahydrin, Metrin, Naqua, Spenzide, Triazide, Trichlormas*
Multi-ingredient drugs: Metatensin, Naquival, Ropres
Usual dose: 2–4 mg per day

Trichlormethiazide may be used to relieve fluid accumulation in the tissues. Another use is to bring high blood pressure levels down toward normal. In many instances trichlormethiazide is effective alone. When used with another blood-pressure-reducing drug, however, the effect can be greater than the sum of the two drugs.

This drug may exert a variety of side effects. These occur in the stomach and digestive tract, the nervous system, the skin, and other parts of the body. Examples of side effects that may impair flying ability include diarrhea, dizziness, nausea, vomiting, headache, and weakness.

The half-life of trichlormethiazide is about six hours. Most of the drug is cleared from the body within two days following discontinuation of use.

Consult the FAA for approval to continue piloting while taking trichlormethiazide. If it is being used in combination with another blood-pressure-reducing drug, flying may not be approved due to the additional drug. Additionally, the condition for which the treatment is given may preclude safe piloting.

Chapter 8

Category IV Drugs: Flight Duties Are Not Permissible Until Drug Treatment Has Been Discontinued

Flight activities are not permissible while taking any of the drugs in this category until the drug treatment has been discontinued and the drug is essentially cleared from the body. Individual drug listings here provide information on half-life, or the time needed to achieve significant clearance from the body. For drugs in this category, use three times the half-life to estimate the time needed for essential clearance.

Refer to the drug listings here for more specific information about a drug's effects on flight activities. As always, consult an AME or the FAA if any question remains about the advisability of flying while taking one of these drugs.

Generic name: *allobarbital*
Multi-ingredient drugs: Dialog, Quiess
Usual dose: 180–360 mg per day

Allobarbital is a member of the barbiturate group of drugs. It is used to lessen excited feelings and to promote relaxation through a quieter nervous state.

While the medicinal effects of allobarbital may be beneficial, its side effects are not consistent with the alert state required of pilots. Drowsiness may accompany use of allobarbital, and mental alertness may be dulled.

Suspend flying while taking allobarbital. The half-life of allobarbital is forty-two hours. To clear the body adequately wait five days after the last dose before returning to flight duties.

Generic name: *aminophylline*
Brand names: *Aminodur, Lixamol, Somophyllin*
Multi-ingredient drugs: Ambesed, Amephytal, Amesec, Am-Phed, Asmakirk, Asmicone, Azmadrine, Dainite, Dayllin, Deprol, Roamphed
Usual dose: (varies)

Aminophylline is used to prevent and treat the symptoms of asthma and related respiratory ailments. It eases breathing and enhances the circulation and oxygenation of blood in the lungs.

In addition to its intended therapeutic effects, aminophylline may cause adverse side effects. Examples of side effects that are of significance to pilots include headache, restlessness, rapid heart rate, nausea, vomiting, pain in the upper abdomen, and diarrhea.

The half-life of aminophylline is about four hours. Allow twelve hours after the last dose to clear most of the drug from the body.

Flying should be suspended while taking aminophylline. The condition for which the drug is being taken may preclude safe piloting duties. Consult an AME about flight duties when aminophylline is prescribed.

Generic name: *amobarbital*
Brand name: *Amytal*
Multi-ingredient drugs: Amcord, Amobell, Amodex, Arcodex, Butatrax, Dexam, Dexamyl, Dexol, Duffa Barb, Ectasule, Gastel, Medral, Tedfern, Tuinal
Usual dose: (varies)

Amobarbital is a member of the barbiturate family. It is used to calm an excited individual and to aid induction of sleep. It is a commonly abused drug.

In addition to its therapeutic effect, amobarbital may cause adverse side effects. Some of these side effects that are of significance to pilots are "sleep hangover," decreased mental alertness, and headache.

The half-life of amobarbital is about thirty hours. It takes five days from the last dose of amobarbital to its eventual clearance from the body.

A user of amobarbital should suspend flight duties. If in doubt about a safe return to flight duties, consult an AME.

Generic name: *azatadine*
Brand name: *Optimine*
Usual dose: 2–4 mg per day

Azatadine is an antihistamine used to treat the symptoms of allergic hay fever and hives.

In addition to its desired therapeutic effects unwanted side effects may occur, including sleepiness, dizziness, loss of coordination, and upper abdominal discomfort.

Suspend flight activities when azatadine is prescribed. When the acute allergic condition is over, wait twenty-four hours from the time of the last dose of the drug prior to resuming flight duties.

Generic name: *barbital*
Multi-ingredient drugs: Barbatose, Elixsed, Nevratose, Pascotal, Plexonal, Sevocol
Usual dose: (varies)

Barbital is a member of the barbiturate group. It is used to calm the nerves and also to induce sleep.

In addition to its beneficial therapeutic effect, barbital may cause unwanted side effects. And because it is a member of the barbiturate group, it is subject to drug abuse. Examples of side effects that are of significance to pilots include drowsiness, skin rash, abdominal discomfort, and lessened mental alertness.

Suspend flight activities while taking barbital. Allow forty-eight hours from the last dose to clear the body of the drug and to overcome the hangover effects. If in doubt about a return to flight duties, consult an AME.

Generic name: *buclizine*
Brand name: *Bucladin*
Usual dose: 50–100 mg per day

Buclizine is used to help relieve motion sickness. It aids in preventing the nausea, vomiting, and dizziness of motion sickness that are very disabling.

The side effects that may arise from using buclizine are drowsiness and decreased alertness.

Suspend flight duties while taking buclizine. The half-life of buclizine is about eight hours. Allow twenty-four hours after the last dose before

103

resumption of flight. This will permit a substantial clearance of the drug from the body.

Generic name: *butabarbital*
Brand names: *Butahab, Butal, Butatran*
Multi-ingredient drugs: Asmadil, Buden, Butizide, Dolonil, Pedo-sol, Pepo-Sol, Quibron Plus, Sterabron, Teolar, Trimsulex
Usual dose: 45–50 mg per day

Butabarbital is a member of the barbiturate group and is subject to abuse. It is used to reduce an overexcited state, allay nervousness, and promote sleep. It can produce a significant hangover effect.

In addition to its desired effects, butabarbital may give rise to adverse side effects. These include nausea and dizziness.

The medical effects of the drug decrease piloting ability, as do the side effects. Butabarbital causes a significant drop in mental alertness.

Suspend flight activities while taking butabarbital. The half-life of butabarbital is about thirty hours. To allow clearance of the drug from the body, wait four days from the last dose.

Generic name: *butalbital*
Multi-ingredient drugs: Al-Nal, Arbutal, Coli-Inel, Fiorinal, Fiosal, Isollyl, Lessten, Obamide, Plexonal, Tensobarb
Usual dose: 200–300 mg per day

Butalbital in combination with other pain-relieving drugs such as aspirin and acetaminophen is used to treat tension headaches and stiff muscles in the neck and shoulder.

Butalbital is a member of the barbiturate group. It may become habit-forming. It is also subject to abuse. There are unwanted side effects that accompany butalbital's therapeutic effects; these are drowsiness and loss of alertness.

Flight duties should be suspended while taking butalbital. Consult an AME in regard to future pilot duties when a condition exists that requires treatment by butalbital. It takes several days for the drug to be cleared from the body following the last dose.

Generic name: *clidinium*
Brand name: *Quarzan*
Usual dose: 15–20 mg per day

Clidinium is used in the treatment of peptic ulcers. It reduces the contractions of the stomach muscles and decreases the amount of acid secreted into the stomach.

In addition to its desired therapeutic effects, clidinium may cause unwanted side effects. Examples of these side effects that are of significance to pilots are drowsiness, blurred vision, headache, and mental confusion.

Flying should be suspended while taking clidinium, not only because of the drug's side effects but also because the condition being treated may preclude safe pilot duties.

Most of the drug will be cleared from the body within two days after its discontinuation. Consult an AME about resuming flight duties.

Generic name: *codeine*
Usual dose: (varies)

Codeine is used to suppress coughing and for the relief of moderate to severe pain. It is derived from opium and is subject to abuse.

In addition to its desired therapeutic effect, codeine may cause adverse side effects. Examples of these side effects that are significant to pilots include dizziness, constipation, mental confusion, and nausea.

The half-life of codeine is about four hours. Allow twelve hours between the final dose of codeine and the resumption of flight activities. This will essentially clear the body of the drug.

Suspend flight activities while using codeine. Its effects are disabling for a pilot. If in doubt about the status of the original condition and its possible adverse effect on piloting, consult an AME.

Generic name: *cyclizine*
Brand name: *Marezine*
Usual dose: up to about 200 mg per day

Cyclizine is used to help relieve the effects of motion sickness by preventing the symptomatic nausea, vomiting, and dizziness that may be very disabling.

The unwanted side effects that may arise from using cyclizine are drowsiness and lessened alertness. For a pilot this presents a dilemma:

the effects of motion sickness are disabling; the side effects of cyclizine, however, even if the motion sickness is controlled, may diminish the mental alertness needed in flying.

Suspend flight activities while taking cyclizine.

The half-life of cyclizine is about two hours. Allow at least six hours between the last dose of cyclizine and the resumption of flying.

Generic name: *dextromethorphan*
Usual dose: up to 120 mg per day

Dextromethorphan is a cough suppressant. Like codeine, it controls coughing, but it lacks many of codeine's narcotic side effects.

Dextromethorphan is usually taken in the form of a cough or cold preparation with a number of other ingredients. It is one of the most commonly used cough-controlling drugs found in over-the-counter preparations. Its presence in a preparation can be verified by reading the list of active ingredients given on the label.

The adverse side effects that accompany use of dextromethorphan must be considered along with those of the other ingredients of each preparation. In addition, the condition for which the drug is taken may temporarily preclude safe piloting duties.

The half-life of dextromethorphan is about four hours. It takes one day from the last dose of dextromethorphan to its essential clearance from the body.

When use of a preparation containing dextromethorphan begins, suspend flight activities. Consult an AME about a return to duty.

Generic name: *dicyclomine*
Brand names: *Antispas, Bellatal, Benomine, Bentyl, Cyclonil, Cyclospas, Cycotyl, Dibent, Diomine, Di-Spaz, Dyspas, Klomine, Nospaz, Pem-Spaz, Rotyl, Spascol, Spastran, Spastyl*
Usual dose: 30–80 mg per day

Dicyclomine works to reduce the contractions of smooth muscle in the digestive tract. This drug is used in the treatment of ulcers and other ailments of the digestive tract.

In addition to its desired therapeutic effects, dicyclomine may cause adverse side effects. Because it may cause drowsiness and blurred vision, users are advised not to drive or operate dangerous machinery. Some side effects that are of interest to fliers are headache, nervousness, weakness, and nausea.

Suspend flight duties while using dicyclomine. When use of the drug is ended consult with an AME about a safe return to flying. The condition being treated may itself preclude safe flight. Twenty-four hours after discontinuing the drug, it should be cleared from the body.

Generic name: *dihydrocodeine*
Usual dose: up to 120 mg per day

Dihydrocodeine is used to provide relief from pain. It also has quieting or calming effects, and it is often subject to abuse.

In addition to its desired therapeutic effects, dihydrocodeine can cause adverse side effects. Examples of these side effects that are of interest to pilots include drowsiness, mental confusion, and lightheadedness.

Suspend flight activities while taking any preparation that contains dihydrocodeine. Check the label of any over-the-counter preparation for dihydrocodeine if there is a claimed pain-relieving effect. When use of dihydrocodeine ends, consult an AME about the resumption of flight activities. The condition for which it is taken may still preclude safe flight unless resolved.

The half-life is about four hours. It takes one day to clear the drug from the body.

Generic name: *dimenhydrinate*
Brand names: *Dimenate, Dimenest, Dinate, Dramabon, Dramamine, Dramanate, Dramanel, Dramate, Dramlin, Dramoject, Dymenate, Keminate, Marmine, Nauzine, Wehamine*
Multi-ingredient drugs: A-Van, D-Vaso, Meni-D, Nicovert, Reidamine, Tri-Vert, Verticon
Usual dose: 200–400 mg per day

Dimenhydrinate is used to relieve motion sickness by preventing the accompanying nausea, vomiting, and dizziness that may be disabling.

The side effects that arise from using dimenhydrinate are drowsiness and decreased alertness. For a pilot this presents a problem; the effects of motion sickness are disabling, but so are the side effects of dimenhydrinate. Even if the motion sickness is controlled, impaired mental sharpness adverse to piloting can occur.

Suspend flight activities while taking dimenhydrinate.

The half-life of dimenhydrinate is about eight hours. Allow twenty-four hours between the last dose and the resumption of flying.

107

Generic name: *dyphylline*
Brand names: *Airet, Bronchofort, Bronkospas, Brosema, Circair, Dilor, Diphylline, Droxylline, Dyflex, Dylline, Emfabid, Lufyllin, Neothylline, Nulin, Panfil, Parbron*
Multi-ingredient drugs: Dilacaps, Dycolate, Embron, Emfaseem, G-Bron, Neospect, Neovar, Parbron, Phyldrox
Usual dose: (varies)

Dyphylline is used to treat certain kinds of asthma, bronchitis, and certain other pulmonary illnesses. It acts to dilate the bronchial airways.

In addition to its desired medicinal effects, dyphylline may cause unwanted side effects. Examples of these side effects that are of significance to pilots are irritations of the digestive tract that may give rise to pain in the upper abdomen, nausea, and vomiting.

Suspend flight activities while using dyphylline. Consult an AME in regard to resumption of flight if in doubt about the underlying medical condition as a safety hazard for pilots.

Allow twenty-four hours for body clearance between the time of the last dose and resumption of pilot duties.

Generic name: *flurazepam*
Brand name: *Dalmane*
Usual dose: 30 mg at bedtime

Flurazepam is used to help overcome insomnia. Some use it if there are frequent awakenings during the night or when awakening occurs too early in the morning.

In addition to its desired sedative effects, flurazepam may cause adverse side effects. Examples of these side effects that are of special interest to fliers include dizziness, drowsiness, and lightheadedness. Mental alertness may be diminished, and much caution is needed in regard to piloting aircraft, driving a car, or operating dangerous machinery when under the influence of flurazepam.

Flying activities should not be mixed with taking flurazepam. If insomnia persists, obtain a medical consultation concerning the condition.

Its half-life is about twelve hours. Allow thirty-six hours between the last dose of flurazepam and the resumption of flight duties.

Generic name: *glutethimide*
Brand name: *Doriden*
Usual dose: .25–.5 gm at bedtime

Glutethimide is used to assist in overcoming insomnia. It is generally used for a short term of one to two weeks.

In addition to its desired sedative effects, glutethimide may cause adverse side effects. Examples of these side effects that are of special interest to pilots include blurring of vision, drowsiness, and hangover. Alertness and coordination may be impaired to such an extent that piloting, driving a car, or operating dangerous machinery should be avoided.

Suspend flying while taking blutethimide. When use of glutethimide is ended, allow thirty hours between the last dose and the resumption of flight activities.

The half-life of glutethimide is about ten hours.

Generic name: *hexocyclium*
Brand name: *Tral*
Usual dose: 100 mg per day

Hexocyclium is used to treat ulcers. It works to decrease stomach secretions and to reduce muscle contractions in the digestive tract.

In addition to its desired therapeutic effects, hexocyclium may cause a significant number of adverse side effects. Examples of these side effects that are of significance to pilots are blurred vision, headaches, dizziness, and weakness. Because of these effects, it may not be safe to pilot an aircraft, drive a car, or operate dangerous machinery while taking hexocyclium.

Suspend flight activities while taking hexocyclium. Twenty-four hours after terminating use, most of the drug is cleared from the body. If the symptoms for which the drug was taken have abated, but there is still a question about the conditions for which it was taken, consult an AME prior to undertaking pilot duties.

Generic name: *loperamide*
Brand name: *Imodium*
Usual dose: (varies)

Loperamide is used in the treatment of diarrhea.

In addition to its desired therapeutic effects, loperamide may cause adverse side effects. Examples of these side effects that are of significance to pilots include dizziness, drowsiness, abdominal pain, and nausea and vomiting.

Suspend flight activities while using loperamide. When in doubt about the effect on pilot duties of the condition for which the treatment was given, consult an AME prior to flying.

The half-life of loperamide is about forty hours. Allow five days between the last dose of loperamide and the resumption of flight activities.

Generic name: *meclizine*
Brand names: *Amvert, Antigo, Antivert, Avert, Bonine, V-Cline*
Multi-ingredient drug: Bonadoxin
Usual dose: 25–50 mg per day

Meclizine is used to lessen or eliminate dizziness, nausea, and vomiting that may be associated with motion sickness.

In addition to its therapeutic effects, meclizine may cause adverse side effects. Examples of these effects that may be of significance to pilots are drowsiness, dry mouth, and blurred vision. Drowsiness and blurred vision may preclude the user from undertaking safe pilot duties, safe driving, or the safe operation of dangerous machinery.

Suspend flight activities while taking meclizine. Although the disabling effects of motion sickness are avoided, the drowsiness side effect is disabling for pilots.

The half-life of meclizine is about six hours. Allow eighteen hours between the last dose and the resumption of flight activities.

Generic name: *mefenamic acid*
Brand name: *Ponstel*
Usual dose: 750–1000 mg per day

Mefenamic acid is used to relieve mild to moderate pain, but its length of use is usually limited to one week.

In addition to its desired analgesic, or pain-relieving, effects, mefenamic acid may cause unwanted side effects. Examples of these side effects that may be of interest to pilots are diarrhea, drowsiness, dizziness, blurred vision, and skin rash.

Suspend flight activities while using mefenamic acid. The condition for which it is taken may preclude safe flight. When use of mefenamic acid is ended and pain is no longer a problem, allow forty-eight hours prior to resumption of pilot duties. Consult an AME when in doubt about the drug or the condition for which it is taken.

110

Generic name: *mephobarbital*
Brand names: *Mebaral, Mephohab*
Multi-ingredient drugs: Mebroin, Reme
Usual dose: (varies)

Mephobarbital is used as a sedating agent for relief of feelings of anxiety, tension, or apprehension. It is also used as an anticonvulsant, either alone or in combination with other drugs.

In addition to its desired therapeutic effects, mephobarbital may cause unwanted side effects. Examples of these side effects that are of interest to pilots include headache, hangover, and skin rash.

Suspend flight activities while using mephobarbital. Levels of tension or anxiety that require use of mephobarbital are disabling for a pilot. The possibility of convulsive seizures is also disqualifying.

Allow twenty-four hours following discontinuation of the drug prior to undertaking flight duties. Consult an AME if in doubt about the underlying condition and its compatibility with safe flight.

Generic name: *methocarbamol*
Brand names: *Carboxin, Delaxin, Forbaxin, M-Axin, Robaxin, Tumol*
Usual dose: 4000 mg per day

Methocarbamol is used in the treatment of painfully stiff muscles along with other forms of therapy, such as rest and physical therapy.

In addition to its desired medicinal effects, methocarbamol may cause unwanted side effects. Examples of these side effects that are of interest to pilots are drowsiness, dizziness, and blurred vision.

Suspend flight activities while using methocarbamol. Consult with an AME about resumption of flying if recovery is not adequate. If in doubt about the status of recovery from the condition for which the drug is taken, consult an AME as well.

The half-life of methocarbamol is about eight hours. Allow twenty-four hours between the last dose and the resumption of flying.

Generic name: *pentobarbital*
Brand name: *Nembutal*
Multi-ingredient drug: Anser
Usual dose: (varies)

Pentobarbital is a member of the barbiturate group. It is used to induce sleep or, in smaller doses, to exert a calming effect. Addiction occurs when pentobarbital is used for a sustained period of time. Also, tolerance develops rapidly, resulting in the need for higher doses to achieve the same drug effect.

In addition to its desired therapeutic effects, pentobarbital may cause unwanted side effects. Examples of these side effects that are of special significance to pilots include drowsiness, hangover, impairment of mental functions, and nausea.

Suspend flight activities while using pentobarbital. The side effects, such as the hangover effect, are disabling for a pilot.

The half-life of pentobarbital is about thirty hours. Allow four days between the last dose of pentobarbital and the resumption of flight activities.

Generic name: *phenobarbital*

Brand names: *Barbikote, Eskabarb, Henotal, Infadorm, Kotabarb, Luminal, Panpheno, Phenagesic, Phenalix, Phenosquar, Quaibar, Sedadrops, Sedatal, Sherital, Solfoton, Solu-Barb, Yelophen*

Usual dose: (varies)

Phenobarbital is used to control various types of convulsions, to exert a calming effect, and to assist in overcoming insomnia. It is also used in medicines that quiet an overactive stomach, as in peptic ulcer cases.

In addition to its desired therapeutic effect, phenobarbital may cause unwanted side effects. Examples of these side effects that are of significance to pilots include drowsiness, loss of mental alertness, dizziness, and diarrhea. It is subject to abuse.

Suspend flight activities while using phenobarbital.

The half-life of phenobarbital is about six days. Allow eighteen days from the last dose to clear the body of the drug.

Consult an AME about future flight duties when phenobarbital has been prescribed.

Generic name: *prednisolone*
Brand names: *Aqualone, Biopred, Co-Pred, Co-Prelone, Cordrol, Coto-gesic, Delcort, Econopred, Fernisolone, Hydeltrasol, Lonetabs, Meda-cort, Meticortelone, Meti-Derm, Metreton, Milone, Predalone, Pred-cor, Prednisol, Prednoral, Pricortin, Ropredlone, Ru-Cort, Savacort, Steralone, Sterane, Ulacort*
Multi-ingredient drugs: Cetapred, Delta-Cortef, Metimyd, Neo-Hydel-trasol, Optimyd
Usual dose: (varies)

Prednisolone is used to treat a wide variety of conditions that will respond to the antiinflammatory effects of this steroid-type drug.

In addition to its desired therapeutic effects, prednisolone may cause a wide range of adverse side effects. Examples of these side effects that are of significance to pilots include weakness, headache, skin rash, mental confusion, and nausea.

The half-life of prednisolone is about eight hours. It takes twenty-four hours from the last dose of prednisolone to its essential clearance from the body. Several additional days (in some cases weeks) may be necessary for certain side effect changes to return to normal.

Suspend flight activities while using prednisolone. Consult an AME or the FAA in regard to future flight activities when prednisolone has been prescribed.

Generic name: *prednisone*
Brand names: *Am-Forte, Cortan, Delta-Dome, Deltasone, Fernisone, Halcorten, Lisacort, Meticorten, New Panora Trace, Orasone, Pred-nagen, Prednicen M, Prednirich, Ropred, Sterapred*
Usual dose: (varies)

Prednisone is a member of the steroid group. It is used to treat a wide variety of ailments, including joint inflammations, allergies, and hyper-sensitivities.

In addition to its desired therapeutic effects, prednisone can cause a wide variety of unwanted side effects. Examples of these side effects that are of interest to pilots include weakness, mental confusion, dizziness, headache, and fluid accumulation in the tissues.

Suspend all flight activities while using prednisone. Consult an AME or the FAA about future pilot activities when a condition exists requiring prednisone.

Generic name: *promethazine*
Brand names: *Anergan, Co-Gen, Dorme, Fenazine, Historest, Lempro-meth, Medergan, Methazine, Methigan, Phencen, Phenerex, Phener-gan, Phenerhist, Phenmar, Pro-Meth, Promethanead, Promethastan, Promine, Promocot, Provigan, Prozine, Quadnite, Rola-Methazine, Shogan, Temergan, Thedameth, Therameth, Visterax, Winazine*
Usual dose: (varies)

Promethazine is used to treat symptoms of allergy, motion sickness, nausea, and vomiting. It also is prescribed to promote a mentally calm-ing effect.

In addition to its desired therapeutic effects, promethazine may cause a number of unwanted side effects. Examples of these side effects that are of interest to pilots include dizziness, blurring of vision, and a di-minished mental alertness.

Suspend flight activities while taking promethazine. The drowsiness or loss of mental alertness that may accompany it are disabling for a pilot. When use of promethazine is ended, allow two days for clearance of the drug from the body and the disappearance of its aftereffects. The condition for which the drug is taken may, if still present, pre-clude safe flight.

Consult an AME when in doubt about flight duties.

Generic name: *secobarbital*
Brand name: *Seconal*
Multi-ingredient drug: Tuinal
Usual dose: 100 mg at bedtime

Secobarbital is used most commonly to assist persons in getting to sleep. It may also be used to provide calming effects. It is subject to abuse.

In addition to its desired therapeutic effects, secobarbital may cause adverse side effects. Examples of these side effects that are of interest to pilots include hangover, drowsiness, lessened mental alertness, head-ache, and nausea.

Suspend flight activities while using secobarbital. Consult an AME if in doubt about a return to flight duty after secobarbital use has ended.

The half-life of secobarbital is about twelve hours. It takes two-and-one-half days from the last dose to the time of the drug's clearance from the body.

114

Generic name: *thiethylperazine*
Brand name: *Torecan*
Usual dose: 10–30 mg per day

Thiethylperazine is used to treat nausea, vomiting, and dizziness.

In addition to its desired therapeutic effect, thiethylperazine can cause unwanted side effects. Examples of these side effects that are of interest to pilots include drowsiness, blurred vision, and weakness.

Suspend piloting duties while taking thiethylperazine. Allow two days from the time of the last dose to the drug's essential clearance from the body. If the symptoms are gone at that time, flight duties can be resumed. If in doubt, consult an AME.

Generic name: *thiopental*
Brand name: *Pentothal*
Usual dose: (varies)

Thiopental is a quick-acting drug that is used to induce sleep or to relieve pain. It is given by intravenous injection in a controlled setting such as a clinic or a hospital.

In addition to its desired anesthetic effect, thiopental can cause adverse side effects. An example of a side effect that is of significance to pilots is persistent drowsiness.

Suspend all flight activities when thiopental has been administered. In practice, there is little choice because it is invariably used in a controlled setting.

The half-life of thiopental is about eight hours. Allow twenty-four hours from the last use of thiopental to a resumption of flight activities.

Generic name: *trimeprazine*
Brand name: *Temaril*
Usual dose: 10 mg per day

Trimeprazine is an antihistamine. It is used to treat hives, itching, and other allergic conditions.

In addition to its desired medicinal effect, trimeprazine can cause unwanted side effects. Examples of these side effects that are of interest to pilots include drowsiness, decreased mental alertness, headache, and dizziness.

The half-life of trimeprazine is about six hours. It takes eighteen hours from the last dose to eventually clear the drug from the body.

Discontinue flight duties when trimeprazine is prescribed. Consult an AME if in doubt about returning to flight duties when trimeprazine has been discontinued. The underlying condition being treated should improve markedly before resuming flight.

Generic name: *trimethobenzamide*
Brand name: *Tigan*
Usual dose: 750–1000 mg per day

Trimethobenzamide is used to relieve nausea and vomiting.

In addition to its desired therapeutic effect, trimethobenzamide may cause unwanted side reactions. Examples of these side reactions that are of significance to pilots include blurring of vision, headache, diarrhea, and drowsiness.

The half-life of trimethobenzamide is about three hours. Allow nine hours from the last dose to yield the drug's essential clearance from the body.

Suspend all flight activities while taking trimethobenzamide. Nausea and vomiting are incompatible with safe flight, as are the drug's side effects. It is also important to discover what is causing the symptoms of nausea and vomiting for which the trimethobenzamide is prescribed. If in doubt about the safety of resuming pilot duties, consult an AME.

Generic name: *tripelennamine*
Brand names: *Pyribenzamine, Ro-Hist, Wolzamine*
Usual dose: 200–300 mg per day

Tripelennamine is an antihistamine. It is used to treat allergic symptoms such as runny nose, irritated eyes, and skin itch or rash.

In addition to its desired therapeutic effects, tripelennamine can cause unwanted side effects. Examples of these side effects that are of interest to pilots include sleepiness, dizziness, confusion, and blurred vision.

The half-life of tripelennamine is about eight hours. It takes twenty-four hours from the last dose of tripelennamine for it to clear from the body.

Suspend flight activities while taking tripelennamine. If the condition being treated has sufficiently improved and the drug has been discontinued for twenty-four hours, flight duties may be resumed.

Generic name: *triprolidine*
Brand name: *Actidil*
Usual dose: 7.5–10 mg per day

Triprolidine is an antihistamine. It is used to treat the symptoms that accompany allergies such as runny nose, reddened eyes, and skin itch and rash.

In addition to its desired therapeutic effect, triprolidine can cause adverse side effects. Examples of these side effects that are of significance to pilots include sleepiness, dizziness, lessened muscular coordination, and blurred vision.

Suspend all flight activities while taking triprolidine. Its effects are potentially disabling for a pilot. When the allergic episode is over and use of triprolidine is ended, allow twenty-four hours to clear the body of the drug before resuming flight duties.

Chapter 9

Category V Drugs: Condition Being Treated Precludes Safe Flying

Drugs in this category are prescribed for conditions that in themselves preclude safe flying, regardless of their treatment.

Refer to the individual drug listings here for more specific information about how the various conditions requiring these drugs and the effects of the drugs themselves affect flight activities.

As always, consult an AME or the FAA if any question remains about the advisability of flying while taking one of these drugs.

Generic name: *acenocoumarol*
Brand name: *Sintrom*
Usual dose: (varies)

Acenocoumarol is an anticoagulant, a member of the coumarin group. It decreases the tendency of the blood to clot and is used to prevent the development of clots in the blood vessels.

Spontaneous hemorrhage can occur while on anticoagulant treatment, and severe hemorrhage can result under these circumstances should a traumatic accident occur.

Flying must be suspended while using acenocoumarol. The condition being treated precludes safe flight.

The half-life of acenocoumarol is about six days. When anticoagulant medication ends, thirty days are required for full clearance from the body.

Consult the FAA about returning to flight duties. The condition under treatment may preclude safe pilot duties.

Generic name: *acetophenazine*
Brand name: *Tindal*
Usual dose: 40–80 mg per day

Acetophenazine is used in the management of certain kinds of mental disorders (psychoses). The disorders are of themselves disqualifying.

In addition to its intended therapeutic effect, acetophenazine may cause a variety of serious side effects. It will reduce a person's ability to operate certain kinds of machinery, drive a car, or fly an airplane. Drowsiness and faintness may occur.

Because the impact of acetophenazine may be so great, flying must be suspended while taking this drug. When use of acetophenazine ends, consult the FAA about future piloting duties.

Generic name: *amantadine*
Brand name: *Symmetrel*
Usual dose: 200 mg per day

Amantadine is used to treat Parkinsonism and to prevent or treat certain kinds of viral flu infections. For Parkinsonism, amantadine may be used alone or with other drugs.

In addition to its intended beneficial effects, amantadine may cause some adverse side effects. Examples of side effects that are of significance to pilots include mental depression, disorientation, dizziness upon arising abruptly from a reclining position, nausea, vomiting, and confusion.

The half-life of amantadine is about twenty hours. Four days after the last dose, most of the drug will be cleared from the body.

Suspend pilot duties until the viral condition being treated has been overcome and a normal recovery has occurred. Consult an AME when this condition is the reason for treatment and inquire about when piloting can be safely resumed.

Also suspend pilot duties if Parkinsonism is diagnosed. The condition is disqualifying. Consult the FAA about the possibility of future flying duties.

Generic name: *amoxapene*
Brand name: *Asendin*
Usual dose: 300 mg per day

Amoxapene is used to treat persons suffering from depression. It is generally used on a long-term basis, often three to six months.

120

Adverse side effects often accompany the therapeutic effects of amox-apene. Examples of these side effects that are of significance to pilots are drowsiness, blurred vision, nausea, dizziness, and headache.

The half-life of amoxapene is about eight hours. It takes two days from the last dose to the drug's clearance from the body.

Suspend pilot duties when amoxapene is prescribed. The condition for which it is used precludes safe flight, as do the potential side effects. Consult an AME or the FAA about a return to piloting duties.

Generic name: *anisotropine*
Brand name: *Valpin*
Multi-ingredient drug: Valpin-PB
Usual dose: 150 mg per day

Anisotropine is used in the treatment of peptic ulcers. It reduces the muscular contractions of the digestive tract and also decreases stomach acid secretion.

In addition to the desired therapeutic effect, anisotropine may cause adverse side effects. Examples of these effects are diarrhea, dizziness, blurred vision, and drowsiness. Flying must be suspended while taking anisotropine, not only because of its side effects but also because of the condition being treated.

When anisotropine is prescribed, consult an AME about future flight duties.

Generic name: *asparaginase*
Brand name: *Elspar*
Usual dose: (varies)

Asparaginase is used to treat certain kinds of leukemia. It is usually given in a hospital setting, and frequently it is used with other drugs.

In addition to its desired therapeutic effects, asparaginase can cause adverse side effects that can be quite powerful. Examples of some of these side effects that are of significance to pilots include skin rash, fatigue, headache, and irritability.

Suspend all flight activities while using asparaginase. Its effects may be disabling for a pilot, as may be the underlying condition being treated.

Consult the FAA in regard to future flight activities when asparaginase has been prescribed.

121

Generic name: *baclofen*
Brand name: *Lioresal*
Usual dose: (varies)

Baclofen is a muscle-relaxing drug, used to treat muscle spasm, or involuntary contractions, as well as multiple sclerosis.

Along with the desired antispastic effect, baclofen may sometimes cause adverse side effects. The kinds of side effects that are of interest to pilots include drowsiness, dizziness, headache, blurred vision, and nausea.

Because of the nature of the condition being treated, flying is not permissible while taking baclofen.

Consult an AME or the FAA about future flight duties when baclofen has been prescribed.

Generic name: *beclomethasone*
Brand name: *Vanceril*
Usual dose: 42 mcg per inhalation

Beclomethasone is a member of the corticosteroid group. It is used for the relief of asthma.

The most serious adverse side effects may occur in those who have been taking other steroid drugs and have switched to using beclomethasone with an inhaler. After the switch, a severe asthma attack may occur.

Flying is not permissible when beclomethasone is prescribed because of both the condition being treated and the side effects of the drug.

Consult an AME or the FAA about future flight duties.

Generic name: *benztropine*
Brand name: *Cogentin*
Usual dose: 1–2 mg per day

Benztropine is used to treat various forms of Parkinsonism.

In addition to its desired therapeutic effects, benztropine may cause adverse side effects. Examples of side effects of significance to pilots are mental confusion, blurred vision, constipation, nausea, and nervousness.

The half-life of benztropine is about twelve hours. It takes sixty hours from the last dose to the drug's essential clearance from the body.

Suspend flight duties while taking benztropine. Consult the FAA about future pilot duties when benztropine has been prescribed.

Generic name: *biperiden*
Brand name: *Akineton*
Usual dose: (varies)

Biperiden is used to treat various forms of Parkinsonism. It is also used to control unwanted effects that may arise with certain other drugs, such as reserpine.

In addition to the desired therapeutic effects, adverse side effects may arise with biperiden. Examples of these side effects that are of significance to pilots are blurred vision, mental confusion, and mood changes.

The half-life of biperiden is about six hours. After biperiden is discontinued, it takes eighteen hours for most of the drug to be cleared from the body.

Flying should be suspended while taking biperiden. The condition for which the drug is taken may preclude safe pilot duties and be disqualifying. Consult an AME or the FAA when biperiden is prescribed.

Generic name: *caffeine-ergotamine*
Brand names: *Cafetrate, Caffermine, Cafrestat, Ercat, Ergocaf, Ergothein, Lanatrate*
Multi-ingredient drugs: Cafergot PB, Ergotatropin, Migral, Sedagot
Usual dose: (as needed)

Caffeine-ergotamine is used to treat migraine headaches. It is not used on a continuing basis, but when a migraine headache appears imminent.

In addition to its desired effect on a migraine headache, caffeine-ergotamine may cause adverse side effects. Examples of these side effects that are of significance to pilots are weakness, muscle pains, nausea, and vomiting.

The half-life of caffeine-ergotamine is about three hours. It takes a day to essentially clear the body of the drug.

Because of the disabling effect of migraine headaches, flight activities should be suspended while using caffeine-ergotamine or while likelihood exists for a migraine attack. Consult the FAA about flight duties when a diagnosis of migraine headache is made.

123

Generic name: *carbamazepine*
Brand name: *Tegretol*
Usual dose: (varies)

Carbamazepine is used to treat epilepsy. It may be used alone or with other drugs effective against epilepsy.

Carbamazepine is a potent drug that may cause serious side effects. These are severe enough to prevent a user of carbamazepine from safely performing flight duties. Examples of adverse side effects that are of significance to pilots include dizziness, drowsiness, blurred vision, lessened coordination, and mental confusion.

The half-life of carbamazepine is about thirty hours. One week after its last dose, essentially all of the drug is cleared from the body.

The condition for which carbamazepine is prescribed is itself disqualifying, and flying must be suspended while using carbamazepine. When use of the drug has ended, allow seven days for its clearance from the body.

Consult the FAA in regard to future flight duties when epilepsy is diagnosed or carbamazepine is prescribed.

Generic name: *chlorpromazine*
Brand names: *Calmazine, Proma, Promaject, Sonazine, Thorazine, Thoronil*
Usual dose: (varies)

Chlorpromazine is used as a tranquilizer. It helps to control certain kinds of psychotic symptoms. Chlorpromazine can also be used to control nausea and vomiting, and it has a number of other uses as well.

Chlorpromazine causes adverse side effects in addition to its desired medicinal effects. The severity of these side effects depends in part on the amount of the drug being taken. Higher doses have a stronger medicinal effect as well as more severe side effects. Examples of adverse side effects of interest to pilots include drowsiness, some loss of muscular coordination, and a reduced state of alertness.

The half-life of chlorpromazine is about six hours. It takes thirty hours from the last dose of chlorpromazine to its clearance from the body.

Flying must be suspended while using chlorpromazine. Consult the FAA about future piloting duties when a condition is diagnosed requiring chlorpromazine. If the condition is a psychosis, it is a medically disqualifying illness.

124

Generic name: *chlorprothixene*
Brand name: *Taractan*
Usual dose: 100–200 mg per day

Chlorprothixene is a tranquilizer. It is used to control the symptoms of psychotic disorders.

Along with its desired therapeutic effects, chlorprothixene may cause adverse side effects. For example, mental and physical abilities may decline so that driving a car, operating machinery, or flying an airplane becomes hazardous. Side effects of significance to fliers include drowsiness, dizziness upon arising abruptly from a reclining position, and blurred vision.

Flying activity must be suspended while taking chlorprothixene. Consult the FAA about future flying activities when a condition is diagnosed requiring chlorprothixene.

The half-life of chlorprothixene is about twenty-four hours. It takes five days from the last dose to the clearance of the drug from the body.

Generic name: *chlorzoxazone*
Brand name: *Paraflex*
Multi-ingredient drug: Parafon Forte
Usual dose: 2000 mg per day

Chlorzoxazone is used to relieve muscle spasm symptoms. It tends to produce muscle relaxation, relieve associated pain, and allows increased mobility of the affected muscle.

In addition to the desired therapeutic effect, chlorzoxazone may cause adverse side effects. Side effects with this drug are not common, but some may affect flying abilities. Some examples of these are drowsiness, dizziness, and lightheadedness.

The reduced physical abilities that require use of chlorzoxazone usually do not permit continued flying. Consult with an AME after the use of chlorzoxazone is completed for advice on a safe return to flight duties.

Generic name: *clonazepam*
Brand name: *Clonopin*
Usual dose: (varies)

Clonazepam is an anticonvulsant drug. It is used to treat certain kinds of epilepsy. It may be used alone or with other anticonvulsant medications.

125

In addition to its desired medicinal effects, clonazepam may cause adverse side effects. Examples of these side effects that are of special interest to pilots are drowsiness, some loss of muscular coordination, headache, and confusion.

The half-life of clonazepam is about fifty hours. It takes at least eleven days between the last dose of clonazepam and its essential clearance from the body.

The condition for which clonazepam is prescribed often precludes FAA medical certification. Check with an AME before undertaking flight duties during treatment with clonazepam.

Generic name: *clonidine*
Brand name: *Catapres*
Multi-ingredient drug: Combipres
Usual dose: .2–.8 mg per day

Clonidine is used to treat mild to moderate high blood pressure. Frequently, clonidine is used along with another blood-pressure-reducing drug. This allows better control of blood pressure with minimal side effects.

Like some other drugs, clonidine causes adverse side effects along with its intended medicinal effect. Those that may be of interest to pilots include drowsiness, dizziness, headache, and fatigue. After taking clonidine for a time, increased doses may be needed to achieve the desired effect on blood pressure. Increased dosage, however, may lead to increased side effects.

The half-life of clonidine is about sixteen hours. It takes four days to clear the body of the drug following the last dose of clonidine.

Suspend pilot duties when clonidine is prescribed. Consult the FAA about treatment approaches acceptable for a return to pilot duties. Each case is assessed individually.

Generic name: *clorazepate*
Brand name: *Tranxene*
Usual dose: 30 mg per day

Clorazepate is used to relieve symptoms of anxiety that may arise from a variety of causes. It is a tranquilizer.

In addition to its desired therapeutic effects, clorazepate may also give rise to adverse side effects. It may not be safe, when taking clorazepate, to operate dangerous machinery or drive a car; it is certainly unsafe to fly an airplane. Examples of side effects of interest to pilots are drowsiness, dizziness, nervousness, blurred vision, and mental confusion.

Flying must be suspended while taking clorazepate, not only because of the effects of the drug on the individual but also because of the anxiety state. When finished with use of clorazepate, consult with an AME about a safe resumption of flying activities. About four days are required to clear the drug from the body.

Generic name: *corticotropin*
Synonyms: *ACTH, adrenocorticotropic hormone*
Brand names: *Actest, Acthar, Acthron, Bel-Cortin, Cortigel, Cortrophin, Nortrophin, Repocort*
Usual dose: (varies)

Corticotropin is used to stimulate the activity of a part (the cortex) of the adrenal gland to produce hormones affecting many other parts of the body. Corticotropin is a hormone derived from the anterior pituitary gland, and it can give rise to a large variety of adverse side effects. The possible side effects depend on individual circumstances.

The illnesses treated with corticotropin are usually serious enough that safe flying cannot be conducted.

The half-life of corticotropin is about fifteen minutes. Within two hours following the last dose, most of it is cleared from the body.

Consult the FAA about piloting duties if a condition exists requiring corticotropin therapy.

Generic name: *cyclandelate*
Brand names: *Cyclanfor, Cyclorex, Cyclospasmol, Cydel, Cyspas, Cyvasco, Rotrilate, Spasmol, Steraspasmol, Vasospasmine*
Usual dose: 400–800 mg per day

Cyclandelate is used in the treatment of a variety of conditions involving decreased blood circulation in the extremities due to vascular spasm.

In addition to its desired therapeutic effects, cycrimine may cause adverse side effects. It may cause stomach distress such as heartburn or belching. Headache and weakness may also occur.

Flying should be suspended until the physical disability that led to the use of cyclandelate is taken care of. Usually cyclandelate is used

127

on a long-term basis. When the need for it ends, consult with an AME or the FAA about resumption of flying.

Generic name: *cycrimine*
Brand name: *Pagitane*
Usual dose: (varies)

Cycrimine is used in the treatment of Parkinsonism.

In addition to its desired therapeutic effects, cycrimine may cause adverse side effects. Examples of these adverse side effects that are of significance to pilots are nausea, blurring of vision, and weakness.

Flying should be suspended while taking cycrimine. The primary reason is the Parkinsonism, not necessarily the side effects of the drug. Consult the FAA about future flight duties when affected by Parkinsonism and its associated treatment.

Generic name: *deslanoside*
Brand name: *Cedilanid-D*
Usual dose: 1.6 mg per day

Deslanoside is a member of the digitalis group. It is used to treat certain heart conditions.

Deslanoside must be used carefully. The margin between the amount of deslanoside needed to produce the desired effect and the amount that may cause toxic effects is quite small.

The half-life of deslanoside is about thirty-six hours. After treatment with deslanoside is ended, eight days are required to clear the drug from the body.

The heart condition being treated will preclude medical certification by the FAA.

Generic name: *desoxycorticosterone*
Brand names: *Cortico, Desoxco, Percorten*
Usual dose: (varies)

Desoxycorticosterone is used in the treatment of Addison disease, a disease that involves inadequate adrenal gland function.

In addition to its desired therapeutic effects, desoxycorticosterone may cause adverse side effects. Examples of these side effects that are of significance to pilots include the accumulation of fluid in the tissues, headache, painful joints, and feelings of weakness in the arms and legs. Mental aberrations can also occur, including mania.

Flying must be suspended because of the possible side effects and because the condition being treated is so serious.

Consult the FAA in regard to flight duties. Each case must be individually considered.

Generic name: *dexamethasone*
Brand names: *Dalalone-LA, Decaderm, Decadron, Decaject, Decalix, Decaspray, Demasone, Deronil, Dexadrol, Dexaport, Dexone, Dezone, Hexadrol, Maxidex, Solurex-LA, Windrow-LA*
Multi-ingredient drugs: Deksone-LA, Maxitrol, Neodecadron, Neodecaspray
Usual dose: (varies)

Dexamethasone is a steroid drug used to treat a variety of ailments. These ailments may arise from hormonal abnormalities, joint inflammations, certain kinds of skin inflammations, some types of allergies, and many other conditions.

The array of adverse side effects accompanying the use of dexamethasone is as varied as its uses. The severity of these side effects depends on the individual taking dexamethasone, the dosage, and the nature and severity of the condition being treated.

The half-life of dexamethasone is about eight hours. Allow two days to fully clear the system of the drug, although it may take several days or weeks to overcome certain side effects of long-term use.

Because of the wide variety of conditions and dosages, it is not possible to generalize about the safety of continued flight activities while using dexamethasone. Each individual using dexamethasone must be evaluated by the FAA with regard to the safety of flight activities. The condition for which dexamethasone is taken may preclude safe pilot duties.

Generic name: *dicumarol*
Synonym: *bishydroxycoumarin*
Usual dose: (varies)

Dicumarol is an anticoagulant, a drug that decreases the ability of the blood to clot. Dicumarol assists in preventing the formation of clots within the blood vessels (and the extension of clots already present).

The reduced ability of the blood to clot is sometimes medically desirable, but it may have serious consequences in certain circumstances. If a spontaneous hemorrhage or an injury with bleeding occurs, control of the bleeding may require extraordinary measures. It is necessary to have ready access to medical assistance while using dicumarol.

The half-life of dicumarol is about thirty hours. When anticoagulant medication ends, it takes six days to essentially clear it from the body.

Flying must be suspended while using dicumarol. The presence of a clot in the circulatory system and the dangers of spontaneous hemorrhage preclude safe pilot duties. Consult an AME or the FAA about a return to flight status when dicumarol is required.

Generic name: *digitoxin*
Brand names: *Cardox, Crystodigin, De-Tone, Digiton, Foxalin, Purodigin*
Usual dose: (varies)

Digitoxin is a powerful heart drug. It is used to treat certain kinds of serious heart problems.

In addition to its beneficial effects, digitoxin may cause adverse side effects. The margin between the desired dose and the dose that may cause bad effects is quite narrow.

The half-life of digitoxin is about twenty-four hours. It takes at least five days between the last dose of digitoxin and its essential clearance from the body.

A heart condition that requires treatment with digitoxin is serious enough that flying activities must be suspended. Consult the FAA about flight duties when a cardiovascular problem exists requiring treatment with digitoxin.

Generic name: *digoxin*
Brand names: *Cardoxin, Davoxin, Dig-Lan, Lanoxin, Saroxin, Vanoxin*
Usual dose: (varies)

Digoxin is a powerful heart drug. It is used to treat certain kinds of serious heart problems.

In addition to its beneficial effects digoxin may cause adverse side effects. The margin between the desired dose and the dose that may cause harmful effects is quite narrow.

The half-life of digoxin is about eighteen hours. It takes five days to clear the body of the drug following the last dose.

A heart condition that requires treatment with digoxin is serious enough that flying activities must be suspended. Consult the FAA about flight duties when affected by heart conditions requiring digoxin.

Generic name: *dihydroergotamine*
Brand name: *DHE 45*
Multi-ingredient drug: Plexonal
Usual dose: (varies)

Dihydroergotamine has two uses—the induction of abortion and the treatment of migraine headaches.

In addition to its desired medicinal effects, dihydroergotamine may cause unwanted side effects. Examples of these side effects that are of significance to pilots include numbness and tingling of fingers and toes, muscle pains, weakness in the legs, nausea, and vomiting.

Because severe migraine headaches are disabling, flying must be suspended when this condition is present. Consult the FAA in regard to flight duties when a diagnosis requiring dihydroergotamine is made.

Generic name: *dihydrotachysterol*
Brand name: *Hytakerol*
Usual dose: (varies)

Dihydrotachysterol is used to treat abnormally low blood calcium levels. The symptoms that arise from this may vary. The problems may reflect an underfunctioning parathyroid gland.

Blood calcium must be monitored in people who are treated with dihydrotachysterol. The margin between the dose providing the desired effect and a dose that causes adverse effects is quite narrow.

The condition under treatment and the possibility of developing abnormally low blood calcium levels (with resultant muscle spasticity) are reasons for suspending flight duties.

Consult the FAA about a possible return to piloting.

Generic name: *dipyridamole*
Brand name: *Persantine*
Usual dose: 150 mg per day

Dipyridamole acts to dilate the arteries that supply blood to the heart muscles. It is used as long-term therapy for relief of the pains of angina.

In addition to its desired therapeutic effects, dipyridamole may cause

131

unwanted side effects. These side effects may increase significantly with higher doses. Examples of these unwanted side effects that are of interest to pilots are headache, dizziness, and weakness.

The half-life of dipyridamole is about two hours. It is cleared from the body within about ten hours of discontinuation.

Suspend flying while taking dipyridamole. The condition for which the drug is taken precludes safe flight. Consult the FAA in regard to flight duty status when angina is present or dipyridamole is prescribed.

Generic name: *disulfiram*
Brand names: *Alcophobin, Antabuse*
Usual dose: 250 mg per day

Disulfiram is used to assist an alcoholic to maintain sobriety. Disulfiram is not used alone but is rather incorporated with supportive counseling and other therapeutic procedures.

Like other drugs, disulfiram may give rise to adverse side effects. These effects, such as inflamed nerves and attendant pain, may also include dizziness and headache. If a user of disulfiram should take alcohol, the body's reaction is marked. Headache and nausea occur. Vomiting may be severe.

The half-life of disulfiram is twelve hours. It takes three days to clear most of it from the body. Reactions to alcohol, however, may occur during the two-week period following the last dose.

Suspend flight activities while using disulfiram or when diagnosis of alcoholism is made. Consult the FAA about flight duties when a diagnosis of alcoholism is made (or if there is a history of alcoholism) or when disulfiram is prescribed.

Generic name: *echothiophate*
Brand name: *Phospholine*
Usual dose: (varies)

Echothiophate, as a solution to be used as drops, is used to treat glaucoma.

In addition to its desired medicinal effects, echothiophate may cause side effects. Examples of these side effects that are of interest to pilots include a stinging, burning sensation and a tearing of the eyes. The pupillary constriction effect will allow less light to pass through the retina, a potential hazard to night flight.

Suspend flying when echothiophate is prescribed or glaucoma is diagnosed. Consult the FAA about a return to flight duties.

Generic name: *ergotamine*
Brand names: *Ergomar, Gynergen*
Multi-ingredient drugs: Bellatrate, Bellergal, Bellergotal, Bellgotral, Ergobel
Usual dose: (as needed)

Ergotamine causes the blood vessels in the head to constrict and may thereby prevent or relieve the pain of a migraine headache. Ergotamine may be used alone or with other drugs. Caffeine with ergotamine reinforces the effects on the blood vessels and may enhance relief (see listing for caffeine-ergotamine in this chapter). Serious migraine attacks may cause nausea or vomiting, and the inclusion of a barbiturate or belladonna may lessen these other effects.

In addition to the desired medicinal effect, ergotamine may cause adverse side effects. Some examples of these side effects that are of interest to pilots include nausea, vomiting, diarrhea, muscle weakness, and muscle pains.

The half-life of ergotamine is about three hours. Eighteen hours after the last dose of ergotamine, most will have been cleared from the body.

Suspend flight activities while using ergotamine or while the likelihood of a migraine attack persists. Consult the FAA about flight duties when a migraine headache is diagnosed or ergotamine is prescribed.

Generic name: *erythrityl tetranitrate*
Brand names: *Anginar, Cardilate*
Usual dose: (as needed)

Erythrityl tetranitrate acts to dilate the blood vessels (coronary arteries) that supply the heart muscle. The increased oxygen supply when additional coronary blood flow occurs serves to relieve angina pectoris resulting from coronary spasm.

In addition to the desired effects of increasing blood supply to the heart, erythrityl tetranitrate may cause adverse side effects. These side effects include flushing of the skin, headache (sometimes severe and persistent), dizziness, and weakness.

The half-life of erythrityl tetranitrate is about fifteen minutes. It takes about two hours to clear the body following the last dose.

Suspend flight activities when angina pectoris is suspected or diagnosed. An angina attack may be disabling during flight. It may also be a forerunner of a heart attack.

Consult the FAA about the resumption of flight duties when angina pectoris has been diagnosed or erythrityl tetranitrate is prescribed.

Generic name: *ethosuximide*
Brand name: *Zarontin*
Usual dose: (varies)

Ethosuximide is a drug used to treat a certain kind of epilepsy referred to as *petit mal*.

In addition to its therapeutic action, ethosuximide may cause adverse side effects. Examples of these side effects that are of significance to pilots include drowsiness, dizziness, nausea, and vomiting.

Suspend flying when ethosuximide is prescribed or when a history or diagnosis of epilepsy exists. Epileptic seizures are disabling for a flier.

Consult the FAA about future pilot duties under the above circumstances.

Generic name: *ethotoin*
Brand name: *Peganone*
Usual dose: 2–3 gm per day

Ethotoin is an anticonvulsant drug. It is generally used to treat epileptics who have the *grand mal* condition. Ethotoin is sometimes used for treatment of other conditions characterized by convulsive seizures as well.

In addition to its therapeutic effect, ethotoin may cause adverse side reactions. Examples of these side reactions that are of interest to pilots are nausea, vomiting, fatigue, dizziness, and headache.

Suspend flight activities while taking ethotoin. A history or diagnosis of epilepsy is disqualifying for medical certification, whether treated or untreated.

Consult the FAA about the possibility of a future return to flight duties.

Generic name: *fludrocortisone*
Brand name: *Florinef*
Usual dose: .1 mg per day

Fludrocortisone is used to treat Addison disease as well as other aspects of ailments caused by underfunctioning adrenal glands.

In addition to its desired therapeutic effects, fludrocortisone may cause adverse side effects. Examples that are of interest to pilots are weakness, possible convulsions, mental disturbances, and headache.

Because of the severity of the condition for which fludrocortisone is used, suspend flight activities while using this drug.

Consult the FAA about the possibility of returning to pilot duties at a subsequent time. Each case is individually assessed.

Generic name: *fluoxymesterone*
Brand names: *Android-F, Halotestin, Ora-Testryl*
Usual dose: (varies)

Fluoxymesterone is a hormone preparation. It is used to counteract a deficiency of androgenic (male) hormones, including testosterone, and to maintain male-associated characteristics. Some weightlifters have used this drug to develop larger skeletal muscle mass. Some female athletes have taken it in an attempt to enhance performance. Certain kinds of cancer of female organs have been treated with the drug.

In addition to its desired medicinal effects fluoxymesterone may cause adverse side effects. Examples of these that may be of interest to pilots include acne, edema, jaundice, and various effects on secondary sex characteristics. It may also promote the development of coronary heart disease.

The half-life of fluoxymesterone is about eighteen hours. Within four days following discontinuation of the drug, most of the drug will be cleared from the body. Male-enhanced bodily changes (e.g., increased facial hair, enlarged skeletal muscle size, deepened voice) may take months or longer to reverse.

Users of fluoxymesterone must be evaluated on an individual basis before flying. Consult the FAA prior to undertaking pilot duties when using fluoxymesterone. The condition for which treatment is given may preclude safe flight duties.

Generic name: *fluphenazine*
Brand names: *Permitil, Prolixin*
Usual dose: (varies)

Fluphenazine is used to treat individuals with psychotic mental disorders, including schizophrenia.

In addition to its desired therapeutic effects, fluphenazine may cause side effects. Examples of these that are of special significance to pilots

135

include decreased muscular coordination, drowsiness, headache, and blurred vision. Individuals taking fluphenazine should not drive a car or operate dangerous machinery because of the possibility of lessened mental alertness.

Suspend piloting while taking fluphenazine. The presence of the mental disorder as well as the adverse side effects of the drug warrant grounding. When fluphenazine use is ended consult the FAA about the possible resumption of flying duties.

Generic name: *glycopyrrolate*
Brand name: *Robinul*
Multi-ingredient drug: Robinul PH
Usual dose: 2 mg per day

Glycopyrrolate is used to assist in the treatment of peptic ulcers.

In addition to its desired medicinal effects, glycopyrrolate may cause unwanted side effects. Examples of these side effects that are of special interest to pilots are blurred vision, headache, nervousness, and nausea. Driving a car or operating dangerous machinery may not be safe because of lessened alertness. Piloting an aircraft while taking the medication is unsafe as well.

Suspend flying while taking glycopyrrolate. The presence of an ulcer may itself be disabling during flight. When the ulcer is no longer a problem and the use of glycopyrrolate is ended, consult with an AME about the resumption of pilot activities.

Generic name: *homatropine*
Brand names: *Homapin, Malcotran, Ru-Spas, Sed-Tens*
Multi-ingredient drugs: Altropan, Bi-Co-Rex, Budon, Hycodan, Mepho-
 bel, Oxagestin, Panzyme, Pasmin, Phenamide, Tolyd
Usual dose: 20–40 mg per day

Homatropine is used to assist in the treatment of ulcers. It lessens the amount of secretions into the stomach and decreases the movement of the muscles of the digestive tract. It is also used to treat diarrhea.

In addition to its desired therapeutic effect, homatropine may cause unwanted side effects. Examples of these side effects that may be of significance to pilots include blurred vision, lessened ability of the pupil of the eye to respond to changing levels of light, headache, and nervousness. Because of drowsiness and blurred vision it may not be safe to drive a car, operate dangerous machinery, or fly an airplane.

The half-life of homatropine is about eight hours. Allow two days from the last dose of homatropine to assure its clearance from the body.

Suspend flight activities until treatment for the ulcer or the diarrhea is completed and the illness has disappeared. Consult an AME in regard to a return to pilot duties.

Generic name: *hydrocortisone*
Brand names: *Acticurt, Alphacort, Cort-Dome, Dofscort, Durel-Cort, Ecosone, Heb-Cort, Hexaderm, Hydrocortone, Lexocort, Lexoderm, Nutracort, Relecort*
Multi-ingredient drugs: Cortin, Derma-Cover, Dermasone, Dermatrex, Dowcortin, Hydroform, Iodocort, Lanvisone, Neo-Hytone, Pricort, Quinsone, Viatone, Viotag
Usual dose: (varies)

Hydrocortisone is used to treat a wide variety of ailments, including primary and secondary adrenocortical insufficiency and rheumatic conditions. It is a highly versatile and powerful steroid drug.

Just as it may have a wide variety of beneficial effects, hydrocortisone may also show a correspondingly wide array of side effects. These side effects depend in part on the nature of the condition being treated and its severity. An additional important factor is the amount of the drug being taken. Higher doses may lead to more frequent or more serious side effects.

Suspend flight activities while taking hydrocortisone. The condition under treatment precludes safe flight.

Consult with an AME in regard to a return to pilot duties when the condition has responded.

Generic name: *hydroxychloroquine*
Brand name: *Plaquenil*
Usual dose: (varies)

Hydroxychloroquine is used to prevent and treat certain kinds of malaria and for the treatment of lupus erythematosus and rheumatoid arthritis.

In addition to its therapeutic effects, hydroxychloroquine may cause unwanted side effects. Examples of these side effects that are of special interest to pilots include headache, dizziness, adverse effects on vision, and spinning sensations.

Suspend flight activities if a condition is diagnosed requiring hydroxychloroquine. The condition for which the drug is used may preclude safe flight. Consult the FAA about possible future flight duties.

Generic name: *isocarboxazid*
Brand name: *Marplan*
Usual dose: 10–20 mg per day

Isocarboxazid is used as an antidepressant. It is prescribed for mentally depressed people.

In addition to its medicinal effects isocarboxazid may cause adverse effects. Examples of these effects that are of significance to pilots include a feeling of lightheadedness or dizziness when arising abruptly from a reclining position, spinning sensations, and headache.

The half-life of isocarboxazid is about six hours. It takes two days from the last dose to the clearance of most of the drug from the body.

Mental depression is a disabling condition for a pilot. When the depressed state is improved and antidepressants such as isocarboxazid are no longer required, consult with an AME about the resumption of flight activities.

Generic name: *isosorbide*
Brand names: *Angidil, Isobide, Isogard, Isordil, Isorgen, Isosorb, Isotrate, Onset, Sorate, Sorbitrate, Vasotrate*
Usual dose: (varies)

Isosorbide is used to prevent or to relieve the pain of acute anginal attacks. As a preventive it may be used in situations likely to produce anginal pain (e.g., exertion, emotional tension, or cold air).

In addition to its desired effects, isosorbide may cause unwanted side effects. Examples of these side effects that are of significance to pilots include headache, dizziness, weakness, and nausea.

The half-life of isosorbide is about fifteen minutes. Therefore, within two hours the body is nearly cleared of the drug.

Flight activities must be suspended because the angina pectoris, the condition being treated, is disqualifying. Consult the FAA about future flying activities when angina pectoris is diagnosed or isosorbide is prescribed.

Generic name: *isoxsuprine*
Brand names: *Isolait, Varisan, Vaso, Vasodigen, Vasodilan*
Usual dose: 40–80 mg per day

Isoxsuprine is used for the treatment of inadequate circulation to the head and brain and for certain other circulatory problems.

In addition to its desired medicinal effects isoxsuprine may cause adverse side effects. Examples of these side effects that are of significance to pilots are skin rash, dizziness, nausea, and vomiting.

Inadequate blood circulation to the brain is disqualifying for a pilot. When this diagnosis is made or when isoxsuprine is prescribed, consult the FAA about future piloting activities.

Generic name: *kanamycin*
Brand name: *Kantrex*
Usual dose: (varies)

Kanamycin is an antibiotic with limited use. It may be used to clear the intestine of certain bacteria before surgery. It is given by injection and may be employed against bacteria resistant to other antibiotics.

In addition to its desired medicinal effect, kanamycin may cause adverse side effects. The most significant adverse effects are possible injury to the inner ear (hearing loss) and to the kidney.

The half-life of kanamycin is about nine hours. Allow at least two days between the last dose and the resumption of flying. Consult an AME about when flying can be resumed.

Generic name: *lanatoside C*
Brand name: *Cedilanid*
Usual dose: (varies)

Lanatoside C is a member of the digitalis family of drugs. It is a powerful drug for use in various heart conditions, including rhythm disorders.

This drug, like other digitalis drugs, requires careful use because the margin between the dose that provides medicinal benefits and a toxic overdose is quite small. Examples of side effects that may occur with lanatoside C include nausea, vomiting, blurred vision, visual color illusions, and heart rhythm aberrations.

Suspend flying when a condition exists requiring lanatoside C. Consult the FAA about future flight duties.

139

Generic name: *levodopa*
Brand names: *Dopar, Larodopa*
Multi-ingredient drug: Sinemet
Usual dose: (varies)

Levodopa is used to treat Parkinsonism.

In addition to its desired therapeutic effect, levodopa may cause side effects. Examples that are of significance to pilots include lessened mental stability, abdominal pain, and dizziness.

The half-life of levodopa is about eight hours. Most of the drug will have been cleared from the body within two days following its discontinuation.

Parkinsonism is a disqualifying condition for pilots. Suspend flight activities when Parkinsonism is diagnosed. Consult the FAA in regard to future pilot duties.

Generic name: *lithium carbonate*
Brand names: *Eskalith, Lithane, Lithonate, Lithotabs, Pfi-Lith*
Usual dose: (varies)

Lithium carbonate is used to treat certain kinds of mental illness having a "manic" component (e.g., "manic-depressive" illnesses). These conditions are also referred to as "bipolar" in nature.

In addition to its desired therapeutic effects, lithium carbonate may cause unwanted side effects, some of which may be eliminated by a change to a lower dose. Examples of these unwanted effects that are of interest to pilots are weakness, lessened muscular coordination, drowsiness, nausea, and vomiting. The therapeutic dose of lithium is often close to its toxic dose, a factor of considerable significance, because it is easy to reach the toxic level when under treatment.

The half-life of lithium carbonate is about twenty-four hours. It takes five days from the last dose of lithium carbonate to clear it from the body.

Mental illness requiring treatment with lithium carbonate is itself disqualifying for pilot duties. When lithium is prescribed, suspend flight activities.

Consult the FAA about a return to flight duties when a condition has been diagnosed requiring lithium therapy.

Generic name: *lorazepam*
Brand name: *Ativan*
Usual dose: 2–6 mg per day

Lorazepam is used to relieve feelings of tension, anxiety, and certain types of depression.

In addition to its desired therapeutic effects, lorazepam may cause adverse side effects. Examples of these side effects that are of significance to pilots include slowed thinking, slowed reflexes, dizziness, weakness, or unsteadiness. It is imprudent to drive a car or operate dangerous machinery, and out of the question to pilot an aircraft, when using lorazepam.

The half-life of lorazepam is about twelve hours. It takes at least three days between the last dose of lorazepam and its clearance from the body.

Feelings of anxiety or depression that require lorazepam are disabling for a pilot. Suspend flight activities while taking lorazepam. When anxious or depressed feelings no longer are present and use of lorazepam is no longer needed, consult with an AME about the resumption of flying.

It should be noted that drug dependence can occur with lorazepam, and it should not be taken for prolonged periods. If the mental condition being treated persists, the condition itself may be a hazard to safe flight and the FAA may request further medical information and studies.

Generic name: *loxapine*
Brand names: *Daxolin, Loxitane*
Usual dose: (varies)

Loxapine is used in the treatment of schizophrenia, a type of mental disorder involving distortions of the perception of reality.

In addition to its desired therapeutic effects, loxapine may cause adverse side effects. Examples that are of significance to pilots include drowsiness, dizziness, faintness, and weakness. It may be inadvisable for a user of loxapine to drive a car or operate dangerous machinery. It is not permissible for a user to fly an airplane.

A mental disorder such as schizophrenia is disqualifying for a pilot. Suspend flight activities when the diagnosis is made or when loxapine is prescribed.

Consult with the FAA in regard to the possibility of future flight activities.

Generic name: *lypressin*
Brand name: *Diapid*
Usual dose: (nasal spray) 1–2 sprays 3–4 times per day

Lypressin is used to treat the symptoms of diabetes insipidus, a disease that causes excessive urine flow and a correspondingly heavy thirst. The disease results from an inadequate secretion of the normally occurring "antidiuretic" hormone of the posterior pituitary gland.

In addition to its desired medicinal effects, lypressin may cause adverse side effects. Examples that are of significance to pilots include stuffy nose, headache, heartburn, and abdominal cramps.

Poorly controlled diabetes insipidus is disabling for a pilot. Suspend flying if the diagnosis of diabetes insipidus is made or if lypressin is prescribed.

Consult the FAA about a return to pilot duties.

Generic name: *mephenytoin*
Brand name: *Mesantoin*
Usual dose: .2–.6 gm per day

Mephenytoin is used to prevent a variety of different kinds of convulsions.

In addition to its desired anticonvulsive effects mephenytoin may cause a number of undesired side effects. Examples that may be of interest to pilots are drowsiness, dizziness, nervousness, and mental confusion.

The half-life of mephenytoin is about eight hours. Two days after the last dose, essentially all of the drug is cleared from the body.

The possibility of convulsive seizures is disqualifying for pilots. Suspend flight activities if a diagnosis of convulsive seizures is made or if mephenytoin is prescribed. Consult the FAA about flight duties when a history of convulsions or of treatment by mephenytoin is present.

Generic name: *methantheline*
Brand name: *Banthine*
Usual dose: 25–50 mg

Methantheline is used to assist in the treatment of peptic ulcers. It quiets the muscles of the digestive system and reduces the quantity of secretions into the digestive tract.

In addition to its desired therapeutic effect, methantheline can cause unwanted side effects. Examples of these side effects that are of interest to pilots include restlessness, a "high" or very good mood, fatigue, and skin rash.

The half-life of methantheline is about three hours. It takes fifteen hours from the time of the last dose to clear the drug from the body.

Suspend all flight activities while taking methantheline. Active peptic ulcers are disabling for a pilot. Consult an AME or the FAA about future flight activities when methantheline has been prescribed.

Generic name: *methylprednisolone*
Brand names: *A-Methapred, Depopred, Med-Depo, Medralone, Medrol, Pre-Dep*
Multi-ingredient drug: Meo-Medrol
Usual dose: (varies)

Methylprednisolone has a wide variety of uses. It is a member of the steroid group and is used to treat adrenocortical insufficiency.

Just as methylprednisolone has the capacity to treat a large variety of ailments, it also has the potential to cause a wide variety of unwanted side effects. An example of the side effects that are of significance to pilots is accumulation of fluid within the tissues.

Because methylprednisolone is so powerful, suspend flight activities while taking it. When use of the medication is ended, consult an AME about resuming pilot activities.

Generic name: *methysergide*
Brand name: *Sansert*
Usual dose: 4–8 mg per day

Methysergide is used in the treatment of certain kinds of headaches that occur frequently and with much pain. Its use is as a preventive agent rather than as treatment for an acute headache event.

In addition to its desired therapeutic effect, methysergide may cause undesirable side effects. Examples of these side effects that are of interest to pilots include chest or abdominal pains, drowsiness, dizziness, and weakness.

The half-life of methysergide is about six hours. It takes thirty hours from the time of the last dose of methysergide to its clearance from the body.

Suspend all flight activities while using methysergide. Methysergide's side effects as well as the condition for which it is used are disabling for a pilot.

Consult the FAA about future flight activities when a diagnosis is made requiring methysergide.

Generic name: *minoxidil*
Brand name: *Loniten*
Usual dose: (varies)

Minoxidil is used to treat high blood pressure that does not respond to other drugs. It is used along with other types of drugs that also help to reduce high blood pressure.

In addition to its desired blood-pressure-reducing effects minoxidil may cause a variety of side effects. An example of the side effects of special interest to pilots is accumulation of fluids within the body.

The half-life of minoxidil is about four-and-one-half hours. It takes twenty-four hours from the last dose to the time of essential clearance of the drug from the body.

Suspend flight activities while using minoxidil. Because minoxidil is such a powerful drug and because incompletely controlled high blood pressure can be disqualifying for a pilot, flight activities must be interrupted.

Consult the FAA about future pilot duties when minoxidil is prescribed.

Generic name: *molindone*
Brand names: *Lidone, Moban*
Usual dose: (varies)

Molindone is used to treat schizophrenia, a severe mental illness in the psychosis category.

In addition to its desired therapeutic effect, molindone may cause adverse side effects. Examples of these side effects that are of significance to pilots are drowsiness, restlessness, blurring of vision, and nausea.

Suspend all flight activities while taking molindone. The potential effects of the drug and the diagnosis of schizophrenia are both disabling for a pilot.

Consult the FAA about a return to flight duties when either molindone is prescribed or schizophrenia is diagnosed.

144

Generic name: *nadolol*
Brand name: *Corgard*
Usual dose: (varies)

Nadolol is used on a long-term basis for the treatment of angina.

In addition to its desired therapeutic effects, nadolol may cause adverse side effects. Examples of these side effects that are of significance to pilots include dizziness, fatigue, headache, and nausea.

The half-life of nadolol is about twenty-four hours. It takes five days between the last dose of nadolol and its essential clearance from the body.

Suspend flight activities while taking nadolol. The presence of angina is disqualifying for a pilot.

Consult the FAA about future flight activities when nadolol is prescribed or angina is diagnosed.

Generic name: *nalbuphine*
Brand name: *Nubain*
Usual dose: (varies)

Nalbuphine is used to relieve moderate to severe pain.

In addition to its therapeutic or pain-relieving effect nalbuphine may cause unwanted side effects. Examples of these side effects that are of interest to pilots include dizziness, confusion, and faintness.

The half-life of nalbuphine is about five hours. It takes twenty-four hours from the time of the last dose to the drug's essential clearance from the body.

A condition producing pain severe enough to require treatment with nalbuphine is disabling for a pilot. When the underlying condition no longer exists and use of nalbuphine is ended, consult an AME concerning the resumption of flight activities.

Generic name: *nifedipine*
Brand name: *Procardia*
Usual dose: (varies)

Nifedipine is used in the treatment of angina pectoris.

In addition to its desired therapeutic effect, nifedipine can cause adverse side effects. Examples of these side effects that are of interest to pilots include dizziness, lightheadedness, headache, and weakness.

145

The half-life of nifedipine is about two hours. It takes ten hours to essentially clear the body of the drug following the last dose.

Suspend all flight activities while taking nifedipine. The presence of angina is disqualifying for a pilot.

Consult the FAA when a condition exists for which nifedipine has been prescribed.

Generic name: *nitroglycerin*
Brand names: *Ang-O-Span, Capnitro, Cardabid, Dialex, Glymar, Hytenco, Niglycon, Nitrobar, Nitro-Bid, Nitrobon, Nitrocaps, Nitrocot, Nitro-Dade, Nitrodan, Nitro-Dial, Nitrodyl, Nitroglyn, Nitrol, Nitrolin, Nitro-Lor, Nitro-Lyn, Nitromast, Nitrong, Nitrostat, Nitrosule, Nitrotest, Nitrotime, Nitrotym, Nitrovas, Nitrozem, Ny-Glis, Progina, Sustac, Vasoglyn*
Usual dose: (varies)

Nitroglycerin is used to prevent and to treat attacks of angina pectoris heart pain attributed to coronary artery spasm.

In addition to its desired therapeutic effects, nitroglycerin may cause unwanted side effects. Examples of these that are of significance to pilots include headache, weakness, and dizziness.

The half-life of nitroglycerin is about fifteen minutes. It takes about one-and-one-half hours from the time of the dose to clear essentially all of the nitroglycerin from the body.

Suspend all flight activities when nitroglycerin is prescribed. Angina pectoris is disqualifying for pilots.

Consult the FAA about future flying activities when angina pectoris is diagnosed or nitroglycerin is prescribed or necessary.

Generic name: *nylidrin*
Brand names: *Arlidin, Rolidrin, Vanidrin*
Usual dose: up to 48 mg per day

Nylidrin is used to treat various conditions in which improvement of the circulation is needed. It acts to open certain blood vessels.

In addition to its desired therapeutic effects nylidrin may cause adverse side effects. Examples of these that are of significance to pilots include nervousness, weakness, dizziness, nausea, and vomiting.

The half-life of nylidrin is about one hour. It takes about five hours to clear essentially all of the drug from the body following the last dose.

Suspend flight activities while using nylidrin. The kind of circulatory problems requiring nylidrin are likely to be disqualifying.

Consult an AME about future flight activities when nylidrin is prescribed.

Generic name: *papaverine*
Brand names: *Biopap, Cerebid, Ceredil, Cerespan, Corpane, Delopav, Diabid, Durapav, Econo-Pav, Genabid, Lapav, Mipav, Pavacaps, Pavacen, Pavacot, Pavadel, Pavadyl, Pavagrant, Pava-Par, Pavatex, Pavatime, Pavco, Vasobid, Vas-O-Span*
Usual dose: 300–600 mg per day

Papaverine is used to relieve inadequate circulation of blood to certain regions of the body, and it may be useful in treating certain irregularities in heart rhythm.

In addition to its desired therapeutic effect, papaverine may cause unwanted side effects. Examples of these that are of significance to pilots include headache, nausea, diarrhea, and drowsiness.

The half-life of papaverine is about two hours. It takes ten hours from the last dose of papaverine to its essential clearance from the body.

Suspend flight activities while using papaverine. The underlying condition and the potential side effects of the drug are disqualifying.

Consult the FAA about resuming flight duties when papaverine is prescribed or a condition exists for which papaverine is indicated.

Generic name: *pentaerythrityl tetranitrate*
Brand names: *Angicon, Angitab, Angitrate, Angitrol, Arcotrate, Baritrate, Covatrate, Dilavas, Hartrate, Kaytrate, Midapet, Pancard, Peaton, Penate, Pentafin, Pentylan, Perihab, Peritrate, Peritrol, Peritryn, PETN, Tetraneed, Tetratol*
Usual dose: (varies)

Pentaerythrityl tetranitrate is used to help prevent development of attacks of angina pectoris. It may be used alone or in combination with other drugs. It is not used to relieve severe pain of angina attacks.

In addition to its desired therapeutic effect, pentaerythrityl tetranitrate may cause unwanted side effects. Examples of these include flushing of the skin, dizziness, headache, and weakness.

The half-life of pentaerythrityl tetranitrate is about thirty minutes. Most is gone from the body about two hours after the last dose.

Suspend all flight activities when pentaerythrityl tetranitrate is prescribed. The presence of angina pectoris is medically disqualifying for a pilot.

Consult the FAA about future flight duties if angina pectoris is diagnosed or if pentaerythrityl tetranitrate is prescribed.

Generic name: *phenytoin*
Synonym: *diphenylhydantoin*
Brand names: *Anelep, Convul, Danten, Diatin, Dihycon, Dilantin, Dileptin, Diphen, Dyphan, Ekko, Etnotin, Span-Lanin*
Usual dose: (varies)

Phenytoin is an anticonvulsant drug. It is used in the treatment of seizure conditions, especially epilepsy of the *grand mal* type.

In addition to its desired therapeutic effects, phenytoin may cause adverse side effects. Examples of these that are of significance to pilots include mental confusion, dizziness, headache, and nausea.

The half-life of phenytoin is about twenty-four hours. It takes five days to clear the body of the drug when it is discontinued.

Suspend all flight activities while using phenytoin. A diagnosis of seizures or conditions that may cause seizures is disqualifying. Consult the FAA about possible future flight activities when either phenytoin is prescribed or a condition is diagnosed requiring phenytoin.

Generic name: *procainamide*
Brand names: *Eclamide, Procamide, Procan, Pronestyl*
Usual dose: (varies)

Procainamide is used to treat irregular heart rhythms.

In addition to its desired therapeutic effects, procainamide may cause unwanted side effects. Examples of these side effects that are of significance to pilots include nausea, hives, chills and fever, and abdominal pain.

Suspend flight activities while using procainamide. The presence of the condition requiring treatment by procainamide is disqualifying for a pilot.

When procainamide has been prescribed, consult the FAA about future pilot activities.

Generic name: *promazine*
Brand names: *Hyzine, Sparine*
Usual dose: (varies)

Promazine is used in the treatment of serious mental disturbances, including various psychotic states.

In addition to its desired therapeutic effect, promazine can cause serious unwanted side effects. Examples of these that are of significance to pilots include drowsiness, loss of some muscular coordination, rash, and fever.

The half-life of promazine is about six hours. It takes thirty hours to clear the drug from the body following the last dose.

Suspend all flight activities while taking promazine. The condition for which it is prescribed is often disqualifying, as are its potent effects.

Consult the FAA in regard to future flight activities when promazine has been prescribed.

Generic name: *quinidine*
Brand names: *Cardioquin, Quinaglute, Quinidex, Quinora*
Usual dose: (varies)

Quinidine is used in the treatment of abnormal or irregular patterns of heartbeat.

In addition to its desired therapeutic effect, quinidine may cause adverse side effects. Examples of these that are of interest to pilots include headache, "ringing" in the ears, disturbed vision, and diarrhea.

The half-life of quinidine is about five hours. It takes twenty-four hours to essentially clear the drug from the body when its use is terminated.

Each user of quinidine must be evaluated on an individual basis for ability to continue flight activities with safety. Consult an AME or the FAA in regard to future flight duties when a condition requiring quinidine is diagnosed.

Generic name: *theophylline*
Brand names: *Aerolate, Aqualin, Asmalix, Bronkodyl, Chur-Phylline, Oralphyllin, Theodur, Truxophyllin*
Multi-ingredient drugs: Asmex, Broncidex, Lardet, Mudrane, Panaphyllin, Quadrinal, Tedral, Verequad
Usual dose: (varies)

Theophylline is used to prevent and treat the symptoms of asthma. It eases breathing and enhances the circulation and the oxygenation of blood.

In addition to its intended therapeutic effects, theophylline may cause adverse side effects. Examples that are of interest to pilots include headache, restlessness, fast heart rate, nausea, vomiting, pain in the upper abdomen, and diarrhea.

The half-life of theophylline is about four hours. It takes twenty hours from the last dose to the drug's essential clearance from the body.

Flying should be suspended while taking theophylline. Consult an AME or the FAA in regard to future flying duties when theophylline has been prescribed.

Generic name: *thioridazine*
Brand name: *Mellaril*
Usual dose: 150–300 mg per day

Thioridazine is used to treat severe mental disturbances, including depression and anxiety.

In addition to its desired therapeutic effects, thioridazine can cause unwanted side effects. Examples that are of significance to pilots include drowsiness, mental confusion, blurred vision, and diarrhea.

The half-life of thioridazine is about eighteen hours. It takes ninety hours (four days) from the last dose to the drug's clearance from the body.

Suspend all flight activities while taking thioridazine. Both the condition under treatment and the potent effects of the drug preclude safe flight. Consult an AME or the FAA in regard to future flight duties when thioridazine has been prescribed.

Generic name: *thiothixene*
Brand name: *Navane*
Usual dose: 20–30 mg per day

Thiothixene is used in the treatment of severe mental disturbances, including psychoses, especially schizophrenia.

In addition to its desired therapeutic effect, thiothixene can cause adverse side effects. Examples of these side effects that are of significance to pilots include drowsiness, faintness, lightheadedness, and blurred vision.

The half-life of thiothixene is about ten hours. It takes fifty hours (two days) from the last dose of thiothixene to its clearance from the body.

Suspend all flight activities while taking thiothixene. The powerful effects of this drug do not permit safe flying. Consult an AME or the FAA if thiothixene has been prescribed.

Generic name: *timolol*
Brand name: *Timoptic*
Usual dose: (varies)

Timolol is used in the form of eye drops for the treatment of glaucoma.

In addition to its desired therapeutic effect, timolol may cause unwanted side effects. Examples of these that are of interest to pilots include eye irritation and adverse changes in vision.

Suspend flight activities when timolol is prescribed. The underlying condition of glaucoma must be controlled before flying can be resumed. Consult the FAA about future flight activities when timolol has been prescribed.

Generic name: *tolazamide*
Brand name: *Tolinase*
Usual dose: (varies)

Tolazamide is an oral medication used to treat "glucose intolerance." It enables a person with tendencies toward hyperglycemia (elevated blood sugar) to consume additional calories without further increases in blood sugar. The drug potentiates the effect of the body's insulin.

In addition to its desired therapeutic effect, tolazamide can cause unwanted adverse side effects. Examples of these side effects that are of interest to pilots include stomach upset, excessively low blood sugar, weakness, and dizziness.

The half-life of tolazamide is about seven hours. It takes thirty-five hours from the last dose of tolazamide to its essential clearance from the body.

Suspend flight activities while taking tolazamide. Hypoglycemic drugs are considered disqualifying by the FAA for pilot medical certification.

Generic name: *trihexyphenidyl*
Brand names: *Artane, Parcotane, Steratane, Tremin, Trihexy*
Usual dose: about 6–10 mg per day

Trihexyphenidyl is used to treat Parkinsonism. Often it is used with other medications.

In addition to its desired therapeutic effect, trihexyphenidyl can cause adverse side effects. Examples of these that are of significance to pilots include blurring of vision, dizziness, nausea, and drowsiness.

The half-life of trihexyphenidyl is about eight hours. It takes forty hours from the last dose of trihexyphenidyl to the drug's clearance from the body.

Suspend flight activities while taking trihexyphenidyl. Parkinsonism is generally a disabling condition for a pilot. Consult the FAA when trihexyphenidyl has been prescribed.

Generic name: *trimethadione*
Brand name: *Tridione*
Usual dose: .9–2.4 gm per day

Trimethadione is used to treat *petit mal* epilepsy.

In addition to its desired therapeutic effect, trimethadione can cause unwanted side effects. Examples of these side effects that are of significance to pilots include drowsiness, fatigue, headache, and dizziness.

Suspend all flight activities when trimethadione is prescribed or *petit mal* epilepsy is diagnosed. *Petit mal* epilepsy is disqualifying for a pilot because it is not possible to predict when a seizure may occur.

Consult the FAA about future flight duties when *petit mal* epilepsy is diagnosed or trimethadione is prescribed.

152

Generic name: *verapamil*
Brand names: *Calan, Isoptin*
Usual dose: (varies)

Verapamil is used in the treatment of angina pectoris.

In addition to its desired therapeutic effects, verapamil can cause unwanted side effects. Examples of these that are of significance to pilots include dizziness, headache, blurred vision, and fatigue.

The half-life of verapamil is about twelve hours. It takes two-and-one-half days from the time of the last dose for the drug to be cleared from the body.

Suspend all flight activities while taking verapamil. The treated condition, angina pectoris, is disqualifying for a pilot.

Consult the FAA when a condition exists for which verapamil has been prescribed.

Generic name: *vidarabine*
Brand name: *Vira-A*
Usual dose: (varies)

Vidarabine is used to treat encephalitis caused by a particular virus, Herpes simplex. It is also used as an eye ointment to treat various eye problems caused by Herpes simplex.

In addition to its desired therapeutic effect, vidarabine can cause unwanted side effects. Examples of these that are of interest to pilots include nausea, vomiting, diarrhea, and dizziness. Use in the eye may lead to side reactions such as a great deal of tearing, burning sensations, and pain.

The half-life of vidarabine is about three-and-one-half hours. It takes about twenty hours to clear the drug from the body.

Suspend flight duties when vidarabine is prescribed. Consult an AME about the return to future flight duties.

Generic name: *warfarin*
Brand names: *Coumadin, Panwarfin*
Usual dose: (varies)

Warfarin is an anticoagulant, a drug that diminishes the ability of the blood to clot. It assists in preventing the formation of a clot in the vascular system or the extension of clots already present.

153

A reduction in the ability of the blood to clot is sometimes desirable for medical reasons but may, in certain circumstances, have harmful consequences. If a spontaneous hemorrhage or an injury with bleeding occurs, control of the bleeding may require extraordinary measures. It is necessary when taking warfarin, therefore, to have ready access to medical assistance.

The half-life of warfarin is about forty-eight hours. When anticoagulant medication ends, it takes ten days to essentially clear the body of the drug.

Flying must be suspended while using warfarin. The presence of a condition requiring this drug, as well as the potential effects of the drug, preclude safe piloting duties.

Chapter 10

Category VI Drugs: Drug's Adverse Effects Preclude Safe Flying

Drugs in this category have significant adverse effects that in themselves preclude safe flying, independent of the conditions for which the drugs are given (though these conditions will likely affect flight duties as well).

Refer to the individual drug listings here for more specific information about how the various conditions requiring these drugs and the effects of the drugs themselves affect flight activities. For drugs in this category, use five times the half-life to estimate the time needed for essential clearance from the body.

As always, consult an AME or the FAA if any question remains about the advisability of flying while taking any of these drugs.

Generic name: *acetohexamide*
Brand name: *Dymelor*
Usual dose: (varies)

Acetohexamide is an oral medication used to treat maturity-onset tendencies toward elevated blood sugar.

The effect of acetohexamide is to lower the level of blood sugar (glucose) by extending the time the body circulates insulin, prior to its removal by the liver. The principal adverse effect that may occur with acetohexamide is an excessive lowering of the blood sugar. This might be brought about by skipping meals and undertaking strenuous exercise. Other adverse reactions include nausea, heartburn, and headache.

The half-life of acetohexamide is about eight hours. To clear the drug from the body, allow two days from the time of the last intake.

As a rule, diabetic tendencies that respond to acetohexamide can be controlled by diet and exercise alone. Discontinue flying when taking the drug.

Generic name: *amitriptyline*
Brand names: *Amtid, Elavil, Endep, Stabanil, Theda T*
Multi-ingredient drugs: Etrafon, Limbitrol, Theda-Tri, Triavil
Usual dose: 75–150 mg per day

Amitriptyline is used to help individuals overcome the feeling of depression. Symptoms of depression may include persistent gloominess, guilt, and low self-esteem.

Amitriptyline and other similar drugs can produce a variety of side reactions. Systems of the body that can be affected include the heart, the skin, and the digestive tract. The list of possible side reactions includes altered blood pressure, increased heart rate, mental confusion, lack of concentration, dry mouth, blurred vision, skin rash, and diarrhea. Of interest to the pilot are the adverse effects of amitriptyline on vision, clarity of thinking, and mental coordination.

The half-life of amitriptyline is forty-eight hours. It takes ten days from the last dose to the time when the drug is essentially cleared from the body.

The need for this drug (i.e., depression) is itself a basis for suspending flight activities. Consult the FAA about a return to flight duties.

Generic name: *amphetamine*
Brand names: *Benzedrine, Bio-Amphet, Robese*
Multi-ingredient drugs: Biphetamine, Delcobese, Geritans, Oby-Rex, Saccamine
Usual dose: 30 mg per day

Amphetamine is used for the treatment of narcolepsy (uncontrollable urge to sleep), hyperactivity, and for short-term support in weight-loss programs for adults. It is highly subject to abuse.

Adverse side effects may accompany the intended medicinal effect of amphetamine. Some examples that are of interest to pilots are rapid, "pounding" heartbeat, dizziness, headache, and diarrhea. A flight of ideas and paranoid thoughts can also occur. Distorted judgment and insomnia often result.

The half-life of amphetamine is about eight hours. It takes two days from the last dose of amphetamine to its clearance from the body.

Because of the potent effects of amphetamine upon the individual, flying must be suspended while it is taken. If narcolepsy or hyperactivity has been diagnosed, consult the FAA about future flight activities.

156

Generic name: *amphotericin B*
Brand name: *Fungizone*
Multi-ingredient drug: Mysteclin-F
Usual dose: (varies)

Amphotericin B is an antibiotic that is used to treat fungal infections. This drug is available as a lotion, ointment, or cream. These are used to treat fungal infections on the skin, where the drug can be applied directly. Serious internal fungal infections are treated with intravenous amphotericin B. In these cases the patients are usually hospitalized.

The adverse side effects of amphotericin B are minimal when it is applied to the skin. With the lotion, ointment, or cream, adverse effects beyond some itchiness are rare. It is safe to fly while using amphotericin B on the skin.

The adverse side effects that may arise with intravenous use may be much more serious and usually determine the extent of hospitalization. For this reason, in addition to the problems associated with systemic fungus infection, pilots must ground themselves when taking amphotericin B internally.

The half-life of amphotericin B is about twenty-four hours. It takes five days to clear intravenous amphotericin B from the body following the last injection.

Consult an AME about when a return to pilot duties is safe. The infectious illness, its response to the drug, and the recovery from the drug's side effects determine when flying can be safely resumed.

Generic name: *atropine*
Multi-ingredient drugs: (many)
Usual dose: (varies)

Atropine has many uses. It may be used to dry excessive secretions in the nose, throat, and respiratory tract. It can quiet the movement of the digestive tract and reduce some secretions there; this may assist in treating peptic ulcers. In the form of eye drops it widens the pupil of the eye. In addition, it is sometimes used in treating organophosphorus poisoning, which may occur in certain aerial insecticide application activities.

Atropine is a potent drug. In order to obtain the desired effect, a variety of side effects often result. Examples of adverse side effects that are of significance to pilots are drowsiness, blurred vision, constipation, and dry mouth.

The half-life of atropine is about thirty minutes. It takes three hours from the last dose to the time of the drug's essential clearance from the body.

Because atropine is so potent, flying often is not permitted while effects of the drug persist. Consult an AME about a return to flight duties when atropine has been prescribed. The status of the underlying condition for which it is prescribed will be a factor in determining that status.

Generic name: *belladonna*
Synonym: *deadly nightshade*
Multi-ingredient drugs: Accelerase, Aller-G, Anusert, Belladenal, Bella-
dol, Bellatol, Bellephen, Bellergal, Bellophen, Bergotal, Bubarbel,
Butabellyn, Comhist, Cystihall, Digestamic, Diozyme, Kinsman's Asth-
matic Cigarettes, Prydon, Solubel, Spasmacaps, Spastoplex, Wigraine,
Wyanoids

Belladonna is a potent drug that may contain several alkaloids (discrete chemical entities derived from a plant). Numerous drug products include one or more of the belladonna alkaloids. The list above is only a small sample.

Belladonna has two major effects. One is a diminished movement of the muscles of the digestive tract. This is helpful in controlling diarrhea. The other effect is a reduction in secretory gland activities. These effects may help hay fever and peptic ulcer conditions. Belladonna also interferes with the ability of the eye to focus and widens the pupils.

Some multi-ingredient drugs may contain only small amounts of belladonna alkaloids in each dose. The half-life of belladonna depends on the half-life of each of the belladonna alkaloids; atropine, for example. The half-life of atropine is about thirty minutes. It takes three hours from the last dose of atropine to its clearance from the body. (See also listing for atropine in this chapter.)

The condition being treated will be a factor in determining the return to flight status. Consult an AME about continued flight duties.

Generic name: *benzphetamine*
Brand name: *Didrex*
Usual dose: 50–150 mg per day

Benzphetamine acts to suppress the appetite and is similar in action to amphetamine. Benzphetamine is used to assist weight-reduction programs for an initial short period.

Along with its desired therapeutic effect, benzphetamine may cause unwanted side effects. As with the amphetamines, it is also subject to abuse. Some side effects of interest to fliers include restlessness, dizziness, nausea, and headache. Insomnia is common, as are a flight of ideas, psychotic thoughts, and impaired judgment.

While taking benzphetamine, flying must be suspended. It takes two days to clear most of the drug from the body after terminating use.

Consult an AME about a return to flight status if in doubt following use of the drug.

Generic name: *bethanechol*
Brand names: *Duvoid, Mictone, Mictrol, Myotonachol, Sterachol, Urecholine, Urolax, Vesicholine*
Usual dose: (varies)

Bethanechol is used to treat certain "nonobstructive" conditions that interfere with the ability to urinate. These conditions may occur after certain types of surgery or after giving birth. There is some indication that the drug may also have beneficial effects in treating certain types of glaucoma.

In addition to the desired therapeutic effects, bethanechol may cause side effects. Some of the side effects that are of significance to pilots include headache, abdominal pain and cramps, diarrhea, and nausea.

The half-life of bethanechol is about three hours. It takes fifteen hours from the last dose to the time of essential elimination of the drug from the body.

Flight duties should be suspended while taking bethanechol. Consult an AME in regard to flight duties when bethanechol has been prescribed. A properly functioning urinary system is necessary for safe pilot duties.

Generic name: *carisoprodal*
Brand names: *Rela, Soma*
Multi-ingredient drug: Sema Compound
Usual dose: 1400 mg per day

Carisoprodal is a muscle relaxant used to relieve discomfort associated with painful muscle-skeletal conditions. Usually carisoprodal is prescribed along with rest and physical therapy.

In addition to its intended therapeutic effect, carisoprodal may also cause adverse side effects. These side effects can be varied. Certain effects of significance to pilots are dizziness, drowsiness, headache, and nausea.

The half-life of carisoprodal is about two hours. It takes ten hours from the time of the last dose to clear most of the drug from the body.

The ability of users of carisoprodal to properly handle flight duties has to be evaluated individually. The decision will depend on the effects of the medication and the condition of the individual. When the condition being treated has disappeared and the drug has almost entirely left the body, a return to pilot duties is permissible.

Consult an AME about flight duties when carisoprodal is prescribed.

Generic name: *cefamandole*
Brand name: *Mandol*
Usual dose: (varies)

Cefamandole is an antibiotic, a member of the cephalosporin group. It is used to treat serious infections that involve the respiratory tract, the urinary tract, the blood, or the skin.

In addition to its desired antibiotic effect, cefamandole may give rise to unwanted side effects. Except for an allergic reaction, these are usually mild and infrequent. Sometimes a skin rash or fever may occur.

The half-life of cefamandole is about one hour. It takes six hours to clear the body of the drug.

Consult an AME about flight duties when cefamandole has been prescribed. The infection being treated may preclude safe pilot duties.

Generic name: *chloral hydrate*
Brand names: *Felsules, Noctec*
Multi-ingredient drugs: Hydra-Hal, Loryl, Neral, Verzone-Sal
Usual dose: .5–1 gm per day

Chloral hydrate is used to allay nervousness and to quiet an excited person. It is also used to promote sleep. It is one of the oldest drugs still in use for these purposes.

In addition to its desired therapeutic effect, chloral hydrate may cause adverse side effects. These side effects are limited to stomach irritation, nausea, and vomiting.

The half-life of chloral hydrate is about two hours.

Flight duties should not be continued while taking chloral hydrate. Allow ten hours from the last dose of chloral hydrate before resumption of flight duties.

Generic name: *chlordiazepoxide*
Brand names: *A-Poxide, Biosed, Brigen-G, Libritabs, Librium, Murcil, Poxi*
Multi-ingredient drugs: Clinoxide, Librax, Menrium
Usual dose: (varies)

Chlordiazepoxide is used to relieve feelings of anxiety and tension. It also may help relieve withdrawal symptoms of alcoholism. It is used to help reduce apprehension and anxiety in people before surgery, especially when local anesthetics are used.

In addition to the desired therapeutic effects, choradiazepoxide may cause adverse side effects. Examples that are of interest to fliers include drowsiness, mental dullness, and euphoria.

The half-life of chlordiazepoxide is about twenty-four hours. It takes five days from the last dose to the clearance of the drug from the body.

Flight duties must be suspended while using chlordiazepoxide. Consult an AME about when it is safe to resume flight duties following treatment with chlordiazepoxide.

Generic name: *chlormezanone*
Brand names: *Fenarol, Trancopal*
Usual dose: 600–800 mg per day

Chlormezanone is used to treat feelings of anxiety and tension.

Along with its desired therapeutic effects, chlormezanone may cause undesirable side effects. Examples of these that are of significance to pilots are drowsiness, rash, dizziness, nausea, weakness, confusion, and headache. A person taking chlormezanone may not be alert enough to drive a car and is certainly taking a risk flying an airplane.

Flying should be suspended while taking chlormezanone. After finishing chlormezanone therapy, consult an AME about resumption of flight duties. Three days following discontinuation of the drug should see most of it cleared from the body.

Generic name: *clotermine*
Brand name: *Voranil*
Usual dose: 50 mg per day

Clotermine is used to diminish the appetite in order to reduce food intake to promote weight loss. On a short-term basis, clotermine may assist in adapting to a smaller intake of food. Many persons resume their old eating habits, however, when the drug is discontinued. It cannot be taken safely for long periods.

In addition to its intended effect, clotermine may cause adverse side effects. It is chemically similar to the amphetamines and may be abused. Examples of side effects that are of interest to pilots include dizziness, mood change, and headache.

Flight activities must be suspended while taking this drug. When use of clotermine is over, consult an AME about how soon to return safely to flying. Three days are required to clear the drug from the body.

Generic name: *cortisone*
Brand names: *Adricort, Cortagren, Cortone, Pan-Cort*
Multi-ingredient drug: Neosone
Usual dose: (varies)

Cortisone is a potent drug, a member of the steroid group. It is used to treat a variety of ailments, especially those having an inflammation component.

In addition to its desired therapeutic effects, cortisone may cause unwanted side effects. Examples of these that are of interest to pilots include weakness, mental or emotional instability, and a greater susceptibility to infections.

The half-life of cortisone is about eight hours. It takes forty hours from the last dose to the essential clearance of the drug from the body.

Each user of cortisone must be evaluated on an individual basis for ability to continue flight duties. Factors to be considered are the nature of the problem requiring cortisone, how much cortisone will be taken, and the length of time that cortisone will be required.

Consult an AME about future piloting duties when cortisone has been prescribed.

Generic name: *cryptenamine*
Brand name: *Unitensen*
Multi-ingredient drugs: Diutensen, Unitensen-R
Usual dose: 2–6 mg per day

Cryptenamine is used to control high blood pressure. It may be used alone or with another blood-pressure-reducing drug.

Like other drugs, cryptenamine may cause adverse side effects in addition to its intended therapeutic effect. Examples of side effects that are of significance to pilots are blurring of vision, mental confusion, nausea, and vomiting. When use of cryptenamine is combined with another drug, the desired control of blood pressure often can be obtained with fewer side effects.

Flying should be suspended while using cryptenamine. It may interfere with the normal vascular response to positive G forces, resulting in loss of consciousness during certain flight maneuvers.

Consult an AME about the resumption of pilot duties when cryptenamine has been prescribed. Most of the drug will have been cleared from the body two days following the termination of treatment.

Generic name: *cyclobenzaprine*
Brand name: *Flexeril*
Usual dose: 20–40 mg per day

Cyclobenzaprine is used to assist in the relief of painful stiffness of muscles. It is usually used along with rest and physical therapy. Besides giving pain relief, cyclobenzaprine reduces tenderness and restriction of skeletal motion. It extends the range of daily activities.

In addition to its intended therapeutic effects, cyclobenzaprine may cause adverse side effects. Examples of these side effects that are of interest to pilots include drowsiness, dizziness, and blurred vision.

The half-life of cyclobenzaprine is about three days. It takes fifteen days from the last dose to its essential clearance from the body.

Because of the adverse side effects, suspend flying activities while taking cyclobenzaprine. Consult an AME about when it is safe to resume flight duties after treatment with cyclobenzaprine. The improvement of the condition under treatment will be a factor in deciding the return to piloting.

Generic name: *deserpidine*
Brand name: *Harmonyl*
Multi-ingredient drugs: Endronyl, Oreticyl
Usual dose: (varies)

Deserpidine is a purified plant substance used to bring high blood pressure down to normal. It may be used alone or in combination with other blood-pressure-reducing drugs.

A variety of adverse side effects may occur with deserpidine in addition to the intended therapeutic effects. Examples of adverse side effects that are of special interest to pilots are drowsiness, dizziness, headache, and nausea.

Suspend flight activities while using deserpidine, as the powerful effects of deserpidine do not allow safe flying. It can take several days to re-adjust the body following discontinuation of the drug, the exact amount of time depending upon the individual and the characteristics of the hypertension.

When use of deserpidine is ended, consult an AME or the FAA about the resumption of flying.

Generic name: *desipramine*
Brand names: *Norpramine, Pertofrane*
Usual dose: 100–200 mg per day

Desipramine is used to help individuals overcome feelings of depression. The feelings associated with depression may include sadness, helpless-ness, low self-esteem, and insomnia.

In addition to its antidepressive effect, desipramine can give rise to adverse side effects. While each side effect does not occur in every person taking desipramine, it is necessary to be alert to the possibility. These side effects can affect the nervous system, the stomach and diges-tive tract, the liver, the blood, various hormones, and other parts of the body.

The half-life of desipramine is forty-eight hours. Ten days following the last dose should see essential clearance of the drug from the body.

The adverse effects that are significant to pilots include drowsiness, headache, nausea, and diarrhea. These and other effects of desipramine lessen one's ability to fly. Furthermore, the need for this drug—the underlying depression—may itself significantly reduce flying ability.

Consult an AME prior to returning to pilot duties.

Generic name: *dextroamphetamine*
Brand names: *Bio-Dexam, Curban, Daro, Del Drin, Dexacaps, Dexa-mine, Dexaphet, Dexedrine, Dexfetamine, Dexime, Dexpro, Dextro-fate, Dofadex, Primacil, Primaphos, Serp-Ex*
Multi-ingredient drugs: D-Anferoid, Dexamyl, Quapitamine, Tega Zol, Thyphet
Usual dose: (varies)

Dextroamphetamine is used in a number of different ways. It acts as a nervous system stimulant. It is frequently used to help dieters lose weight by depressing the appetite, although its effect on the appetite is unfortunately temporary. It is one of the more commonly abused drugs.

Just as its medicinal effects are powerful, dextroamphetamine may cause powerful adverse side effects. Examples of these side effects that are of interest to fliers include insomnia, dizziness, a "high" feeling, impaired judgment, headache, and diarrhea. It also may produce a flight of ideas, agitation, and paranoid thoughts.

The half-life of dextroamphetamine is about eight hours. It takes two days following the last dose for the body to clear itself of the drug.

Because of the effects of dextroamphetamine, flying should be suspended while it is being used. Consult an AME prior to resumption of pilot duties.

Generic name: *diazepam*
Brand name: *Valium*
Usual dose: (varies)

Diazepam is used to relieve feelings of tension and anxiety, and it is useful as well for relieving feelings of stress and apprehension in certain circumstances. Diazepam is also used to assist in relief of muscle spasms.

In addition to its desired medicinal effects, diazepam may cause adverse side effects. Examples of these side effects that are of interest to pilots are drowsiness, fatigue, confusion, and headache.

The half-life of diazepam is about forty-eight hours. It takes at least ten days between the last dose and the essential clearance of the drug from the body.

Because diazepam is a powerful drug and because both its direct effects and its side effects lessen flying ability, flight activities should be suspended while taking diazepam. Consult an AME prior to returning to flight duties.

Generic name: *diazoxide*
Brand names: *Hyperstat, Proglycem*
Usual dose: (varies)

Diazoxide is used to counter low blood sugar levels.

In addition to its desired medicinal effects, diazoxide may cause adverse side effects. The significance of these side effects depends on the condition of the individual. A side effect that is of little concern in some cases may be quite serious where another problem already exists. For example, diazoxide may cause sodium and fluid retention.

The half-life of diazoxide is about thirty-six hours. It takes eight days from the last dose of diazoxide to its essential clearance from the body.

Because of the potency of diazoxide, flying should be suspended while using it. Consult an AME prior to returning to flight duties.

Generic name: *diethylpropion*
Brand names: *Camuate, Novacaps, Novatabs, Tenuate, Ten-U-Mast, Tenuspan, Tepanil*
Usual dose: 75–100 mg per day

Diethylpropion is used to suppress the appetite in people who are trying to lose weight. The appetite suppression is usually short-lived and, therefore, of limited usefulness. Diethylpropion may be abused.

In addition to its desired medicinal effects, diethylpropion may cause adverse side effects. The user may need steadily increasing amounts to maintain the desired effect on the appetite. This may escalate the adverse side effects. Examples of the side effects that are of significance to pilots include nervousness, dizziness, drowsiness, and headache. A person using diethylpropion may not be capable of driving a car or operating dangerous machinery safely and would certainly be hazardous as a pilot.

The half-life is about eight hours. Two days after the last dose of diethylpropion should see its essential clearance from the body.

Suspend pilot duties while using diethylpropion. Consult an AME about the return to flight duties following use of this drug.

Generic name: *diphenidol*
Brand name: *Vontrol*
Usual dose: 100–200 mg per day

Diphenidol is used to treat symptoms of dizziness and some causes of nausea and vomiting.

In addition to its desired effects, diphenidol may cause adverse side effects. Because it is so potent, diphenidol is usually given only under circumstances where the user can be closely followed clinically. Some of the side effects that may be of interest to pilots are confusion, depression, drowsiness, and blurred vision.

Suspend flying activities while taking diphenidol. When the use of the drug is no longer needed, consult with an AME about a safe return to piloting.

166

Generic name: *doxepin*
Brand names: *Adapin, Sinequan*
Usual dose: 75–100 mg per day

Doxepin is prescribed for the treatment of certain kinds of depression and/or anxiety. Some symptoms that respond well to doxepin include anxiety, tension, sleep disturbance, and fear or worry.

Like other drugs of this type, adverse side effects can occur in addition to the desired medicinal effects. Side reactions affect clarity of thinking, the circulation, and the digestive system. Specific side effects can include blurred vision, drowsiness, increased heart rate, skin rash or itchiness, nausea, vomiting, diarrhea, and dizziness.

Because of the underlying mental condition and the possible side effects of doxepin, a pilot should not perform flight duties while taking doxepin.

The half-life of doxepin is about forty-eight hours. It takes ten days to essentially clear doxepin from the body following the last dose.

Consult an AME about a return to flight duties following use of doxepin.

Generic name: *ethchlorvynol*
Brand name: *Placidyl*
Usual dose: 500 mg at bedtime

Ethchlorvynol is used to induce sleep in insomniacs. It is often subject to abuse. It is normally prescribed on a short-term basis (a few days). It may be unsafe for a person using ethchlorvynol to drive a car or operate dangerous machinery.

In addition to its desired therapeutic effects, ethchlorvynol may cause adverse side effects. Examples of these that are of significance to pilots are dizziness, blurred vision, upset stomach, nausea, and vomiting.

The half-life of ethchlorvynol is about twenty hours. It takes four days from the last dose to the drug's essential clearance from the body.

Suspend pilot duties while taking ethchlorvynol. It has the potential for too many strongly adverse effects, and a drug hangover may persist for several hours on the morning after its use.

Consult an AME about the resumption of pilot duties following use of ethchlorvynol.

Generic name: *ethinamate*
Brand name: *Valmid*
Usual dose: 500–1000 mg at bedtime

Ethinamate is used on a short-term basis as an aid in overcoming insomnia. It generally becomes less effective after a week's regular use. After a week of nonuse, its effectiveness may return.

Ideally, drug-free methods should be used by pilots to induce sleep. The use of ethinamate warrants taking certain precautions. Other mental sedatives, including alcohol, may add to the effects of ethinamate, giving a total effect greater than that expected from any one substance. Driving a car or operating dangerous machinery when under the influence of ethinamate also may be hazardous.

Suspend flight duties while using ethinamate. The potent effects of ethinamate are not consistent with safe flying. Two days from the last dose are necessary to clear most of the drug from the body. When use of ethinamate is ended, consult with an AME about a safe resumption of flight activities.

Generic name: *fenfluramine*
Brand name: *Pondimin*
Usual dose: (varies)

Fenfluramine is used to assist dieters in losing weight by diminishing the appetite. After a short period of use (one week), it is often no longer effective. Use should be discontinued rather than increasing the amount, as increasing dosage constitutes a potential health hazard.

In addition to its desired medicinal effects, fenfluramine may cause unwanted side effects. Examples of these side effects that are of significance to pilots are diarrhea, dizziness, headache, and nervousness.

Suspend pilot activities while using fenfluramine. Its powerful effects diminish the mental alertness and coordination needed for flying.

Two days are necessary from the last dose to essentially clear the drug from the body. When use of fenfluramine is ended, consult an AME about a safe resumption of pilot activities.

Generic name: *fenoprofen*
Brand name: *Nalfon*
Usual dose: (varies)

Fenoprofen is a nonsteroid-type drug used in the treatment of certain kinds of joint pains, as in arthritis. It also acts as a pain reliever and helps reduce high temperature.

In addition to its desired medicinal effects, fenoprofen may cause adverse side effects. Examples of these side effects that are of significance to pilots are nervousness, dizziness, nausea, and vomiting.

The half-life of fenoprofen is about three hours. After discontinuation of the drug, body clearance will have essentially occurred within fifteen hours.

The feasibility of continued flight activities while taking fenoprofen must be determined on an individual basis. The severity of the arthritis and the effect of the drug on the individual pilot will determine flight status.

Generic name: *guanethidin*
Brand name: *Ismelin*
Multi-ingredient drug: Esimil
Usual dose: 25–50 mg per day

Guanethidin is used to reduce moderate to severe high blood pressure toward a normal level. It may be used alone or with another blood-pressure-reducing drug. Use of two blood-pressure-reducing drugs may obtain adequate control of high blood pressure with lower doses of each drug and fewer adverse side effects.

Guanethidin causes adverse side effects that may preclude its use. A significant side effect is that of dizzy feelings when rising abruptly from a reclining position. This side effect, called postural hypotension, can cause a pilot to black out when pulling positive G's, as, for example, in a steep turn. Other side effects of interest to pilots include diarrhea, fatigue, nausea, vomiting, blurring of vision, and muscle tremor.

The half-life of guanethidin is variable. Unless side effects persist, the effects of guanethidin are negligible fourteen days after the last dose.

Because of its potent effects, guanethidin therapy is not compatible with safe flying. Suspend flight duties when guanethidin is prescribed.

Consult an AME or the FAA about returning to flight duties after guanethidin treatment.

Generic name: *haloperidol*
Brand name: *Haldol*
Usual dose: (varies)

Haloperidol is used to treat individuals with severe mental disorders.

In addition to its desired therapeutic effects, haloperidol may cause a variety of adverse side reactions. Examples of these that are of special significance to pilots include restlessness, headache, diarrhea, and nausea. Reduced mental alertness can prevent the user of haloperidol also from safely driving a car or operating dangerous machinery.

The half-life of haloperidol is about seven days. It takes five weeks from the last dose of haloperidol to the time that it is essentially cleared from the body.

Suspend piloting while taking haloperidol. The effects of haloperidol are so potent that continued flying is not safe. In addition, the condition for which the drug is prescribed precludes safe flight performance.

Consult the FAA about resumption of flight duties following treatment with haloperidol.

Generic name: *hydralazine*
Brand names: *Apresoline, Dralsine, Rolazine*
Multi-ingredient drugs: Antitense, Apresazide, Apresodex, Apresoline-Esidrix, Dralserp, H-R-H, Hydralazide, Hydrap-Es, Hydroserpasine, J-Hydrap-Es, Pampres, Ser-A-Gen, Ser-Ap-Es, Serpasil-Apresoline, Thianal-R-H, Triazide, Tri-Hydroserpine, Unipres
Usual dose: 50–150 mg per day

Hydralazine is used to control high blood pressure. It may be used alone or with another drug effective in reducing high blood pressure. Two drugs given for reducing high blood pressure often can be used in smaller doses than either used alone. Smaller doses have the benefit of fewer and milder adverse side effects, yet provide the desired control of high blood pressure.

In addition to the desired blood-pressure-reducing effect, hydralazine causes adverse side reactions in some individuals. These side effects often disappear when the dose is reduced. When a serious side reaction persists, the drug may be stopped and a different drug tried. Side reactions of significance to pilots include headache, nausea, vomiting, diarrhea, dizziness, and anxiety.

The half-life of hydralazine is about six hours. It takes two days from the last dose to its essential clearance from the body.

170

Suspend pilot duties when taking hydralazine because of its side effects. Consult an AME about the return to pilot duties.

Generic name: *hydrocodone*
Brand names: *Codone, Dicodid*
Multi-ingredient drugs: Coditrate, Detussin, Hycodan, Hycomine, Hycotuss, Tussend, Tussgen, Tussionex, Vicodin
Usual dose: 20 mg per day

Hydrocodone is used to treat certain types of coughing, especially coughs due to throat or pulmonary irritation. It may be used alone or with other ingredients. It is a narcotic, however, and may cause dependence in long-time users.

In addition to its desired effects, hydrocodone may cause unwanted side effects. Examples that may be of interest to pilots include loss of some mental alertness, nausea, and vomiting. Onset of drowsiness may also make it unsafe for the user of hydrocodone to drive a car or operate dangerous machinery.

Flight activities must be suspended when taking hydrocodone. Do not resume flight duties until the respiratory illness has abated and two days have been allowed to clear most of the drug from the body.

Generic name: *hydromorphone*
Synonym: *dihydromorphinone*
Brand name: *Dilaudid*
Usual dose: (varies)

Hydromorphone is a narcotic substance derived from opium. It is used to relieve moderate to severe levels of pain. It may also be used to suppress coughing.

In addition to its beneficial effects hydromorphone may cause adverse side effects. Continued use of hydromorphone may lead to addiction or abuse. Examples of side effects that are of interest to pilots include drowsiness, lessened mental and physical abilities, dizziness, and mood changes. The drug also promotes constipation.

The half-life of hydromorphone is about eight hours. When use of hydromorphone is ended, it takes forty hours to clear almost all of it from the body.

Because hydromorphone is a potent narcotic, flight activities must be suspended while it is being taken. Consult an AME about the return to flight duties when the drug is discontinued. The condition requiring the treatment may still not be sufficiently resolved for a safe return to piloting.

Generic name: *hydroxyzine*
Brand names: *Atarax, Vistaril*
Multi-ingredient drugs: Ataraxoid, Cartrax, Enarax, Vistrax
Usual dose: (varies)

Hydroxyzine is used to relieve feelings of anxiety and tension. It may also be used for other purposes, such as to relieve certain symptoms of allergy and to help prepare a person for general anesthesia.

In addition to its desired therapeutic effects, hydroxyzine may cause side effects. Examples of these that are of significance to pilots include drowsiness, tremors, and dry mouth.

The half-life of hydroxyzine is about twenty-four hours. It takes five days from the time of the last dose to the drug's essential clearance from the body.

Suspend flight activities while using hydroxyzine. The potent effects of this drug are not compatible with continued safe flight activities. Also, the condition for which the drug is given precludes safe piloting.

Consult an AME in regard to the return to flight duties when hydroxyzine has been prescribed.

Generic name: *ibuprofen*
Brand name: *Motrin*
Usual dose: (varies)

Ibuprofen is used to relieve the effects of rheumatoid arthritis and osteoarthritis. It is also—and now probably more commonly—used for the relief of mild to moderate pain.

In addition to its desired therapeutic effects, ibuprofen may cause unwanted side effects. Examples of these side effects that are of significance to pilots include dizziness, skin rash, heartburn, and blurred vision. Reports suggest the rare development of hallucinations while on the drug.

It is unwise to pilot aircraft while taking ibuprofen, from the standpoint of both the condition being treated and the side effects of the drug. If in doubt about the condition being treated, consult an AME.

The half-life is about six hours. When the drug is discontinued, allow thirty hours prior to performing pilot duties.

Generic name: *imipramine*
Brand names: *Antipress, Imapam, Imavate, Impramast, Janimine, J-Imi-pramine, Norfranil, Presamine, SK-Pramine, Tofranil, Tofranil-PM*
Usual dose: 75–150 mg per day

Imipramine is used to treat the symptoms of depression. These can vary from feeling "low" to serious despair. Feelings of sadness, guilt, and low self-esteem often occur in the depressed person.

Imipramine and similar drugs give rise to many side effects. These may affect the heart and blood vessels, various mental functions, the nervous system, and the stomach and digestive tract. There are other side effects also. The adverse effects of imipramine that are of special significance to flying ability include mental confusion, anxiety, blurred vision, nervous seizures, nausea, and vomiting.

The need for this drug, that is, the state of depression, may in itself disqualify the pilot from flight duties. Suspend flight duties when imipramine is prescribed, and consult an AME. The status of the underlying condition will be a factor given consideration.

It takes eight days between the end of imipramine therapy and the drug's essential clearance from the body.

Generic name: *indomethacin*
Brand name: *Indocin*
Usual dose: (varies)

Indomethacin is used in the treatment of rheumatoid arthritis, osteoarthritis, gouty arthritis, and for a type of inflammation of the vertebrae.

Even though indomethacin may provide beneficial effects hard to obtain with other drugs, it may also cause adverse side effects that may be mild or serious. Examples of these adverse side effects that are of significance to pilots include nausea, indigestion, headache, and dizziness. Some people become depressed while taking the drug.

Do not pilot aircraft while taking indomethacin. The condition being treated and the side effects of the drug preclude safe pilot duties.

The half-life of the drug is two hours. Allow ten hours between the last dose and the resumption of pilot duties.

If in doubt about the condition being treated, consult an AME.

Generic name: *isoproteronol*
Brand names: *Aerolone, Iprenol, Isoprenaline, Isuprel, Medihaler, Norisodrine, Proternal, Vapo-Iso*
Usual dose: (by inhaler)

Isoproteronol is used to relieve difficult breathing that may be associated with asthma and certain respiratory illnesses. As an injectable preparation, isoproteronol is used in the treatment of shock and may be used for cardiac arrest.

In addition to its intended therapeutic effects, isoproteronol may cause some adverse side effects. Examples of these side effects that may be of significance to pilots are nervousness, dizziness, nausea, vomiting, and headache.

The half-life of isoproteronol is about eight hours. It takes forty hours from the time of the last dose to its essential clearance from the body.

Because isoproteronol is so potent a drug, flight activities must be suspended while using it. Consult an AME or the FAA in regard to a return to flight duties when isoproteronol has been prescribed.

Generic name: *meprobamate*
Brand names: *Arcoban, Biobamate, Coprobate, Corum, Desabam, Equanil, Evenol, Mepro-Bev, Meprocon, Meprodan, Meprospan, Meprotabs, Miltown, Neurate, Ostoban, Prebal, Robamate, Saronil, Sedabamate, SK-Bamate, Spantran, Tranmep, Tranqui-Tabs, Tranten, Vistabamate*
Multi-ingredient drugs: Equanitrate, Meprohex, Mepropen, Meprotet, Meprotrate, Milpath, Milprem, Miltragen, Miltrate, Pathibamate, Spasmate, Trimate
Usual dose: 1200–1600 mg per day

Meprobamate is used to relieve anxiety and tension and to promote calm in persons feeling anxiety and tension.

In addition to its desired therapeutic effects, meprobamate may cause adverse side effects. Examples of these side effects that are of special significance to pilots are drowsiness, dizziness, mental confusion, and headache. Meprobamate also may be abused.

The half-life of meprobamate is about ten hours. It takes fifty hours from the time of the last dose to clear the drug from the body.

Because of the potent effects of meprobamate, suspend all pilot activities while taking meprobamate. The condition for which it is taken

174

also precludes pilot activities. Consult an AME or the FAA in regard to returning to flight duties after meprobamate has been prescribed.

Generic name: *metaproterenol*
Brand names: *Alupent, Metaprel*
Usual dose: 60–80 mg per day

Metaproterenol is used to open constricted breathing passages. Usually asthma is the underlying problem, although certain other lung conditions can be to blame.

In addition to its desired therapeutic effects, metaproterenol may cause unwanted side effects. Examples of these side effects that are of significance to pilots are nervousness, very rapid heart rate, tremors, nausea, and vomiting.

The half-life of metaproterenol is about eight hours. It takes forty hours to essentially clear the drug from the body.

Suspend flight activities while taking metaproterenol. It has potent effects that preclude piloting with safety. Consult an AME about the resumption of flight duties when metaproterenol has been prescribed.

Generic name: *methadone*
Brand names: *Dolophine, Westadone*
Usual dose: (varies)

Methadone is used as a substitute for heroin because, although similarly addictive, it does not produce some of the more adverse side effects common to heroin.

In addition to its "medicinal" effects, methadone may cause some adverse side effects. Examples of these side effects that are of special interest to pilots include lightheadedness, dizziness, headache, weakness, and a continuation of the opiate addiction.

Suspend all flight activities while using methadone. All methadone addicts must suspend flight duties because of the adverse side effects of the addiction. The effects of this drug are so powerful that capability of conducting pilot duties is lost.

The half-life of methadone is about fifteen hours. It takes seventy-five hours from the time of the last dose to clear the body of the drug.

Consult the FAA about future flight duties once the need for methadone has been established. Detoxification and recovery from the addiction will be prior requirements.

Generic name: *methamphetamine*
Brand names: *Bio-Metham, Delfetamine, Desodex, Desoxyn, E-Frux, Hydex, Oxadron, Oxydess, Primacel, Semoxydrine, Senostin, Soxyfed, Zemsoxyn*
Multi-ingredient drugs: Alobese, Hysobel, Phelantin
Usual dose: 10–15 mg per day

Methamphetamine is used to assist overweight people in losing weight. It has an appetite-suppressing effect.

In addition to its desired therapeutic effects, methamphetamine may cause certain side effects. Examples of these side effects that are of interest to pilots are dizziness, restlessness, headache, and diarrhea. A flight of ideas may occur also, as may paranoid thoughts. Judgment may be impaired and manic behavior may develop. Insomnia is often a side effect as well.

Suspend flight activities while using methamphetamine. The potent effects of the drug are incompatible with pilot duties. It takes about three days to clear the body of methamphetamine after its use is terminated. When use of methamphetamine is ended, consult an AME about the resumption of flying.

Generic name: *methaqualone*
Brand names: *Quaalude, Soper*
Multi-ingredient drug: Dimethacol
Usual dose: 150–300 mg at bedtime

Methaqualone is used to induce sleep in people who are prone to insomnia.

In addition to its desired therapeutic effects, methaqualone may cause unwanted side effects. Examples of these that are of significance to pilots include dizziness, headache, hangover, and diarrhea. Methaqualone is highly subject to abuse, and dependence may develop.

The half-life of methaqualone is about twelve hours. It takes sixty hours from the last dose of methaqualone to its clearance from the body.

Suspend all flight activities while using methaqualone. The effects of the drug are powerful and are disabling for a pilot. If methaqualone is prescribed consult an AME prior to resuming piloting activities.

Generic name: *methotrexate*
Brand name: *Mexate*
Usual dose: (varies)

Methotrexate is used to treat severe psoriasis and as a component of treatment of certain kinds of cancer.

In addition to its desired therapeutic effects, methotrexate may cause undesired side effects. Examples of these that are of special interest to pilots include nausea, abdominal distress, dizziness, and blurred vision.

Suspend all flight activities while using methotrexate. The strong effects of the drug itself are disabling for a pilot.

If methotrexate is prescribed, consult an AME or the FAA about flight duties. The underlying condition may preclude safe flight.

Generic name: *methyldopa*
Brand name: *Aldomet*
Multi-ingredient drugs: Aldoclor, Aldoril
Usual dose: .5–2 gm per day

Methyldopa is used to control moderate to severe high blood pressure. Frequently it is used in combination with another blood-pressure-reducing drug. When two drugs are used together, this may allow each drug to be taken in a lower dose than if each were used alone.

Methyldopa may cause adverse side effects in addition to its intended medicinal effect. In the first few weeks of methyldopa therapy there may be drowsiness that interferes with mental concentration. Other side reactions may affect the nervous system, blood vessels, liver, stomach and remaining digestive tract, and other organs. Specific side reactions of significance to pilots include headache, weakness, nausea, vomiting, diarrhea, and fever. In addition, positive G force intolerance may occur when taking this drug. The adverse effects of the drug itself preclude safe pilot duties.

The half-life of methyldopa is about four hours. It takes twenty hours to essentially clear the drug from the body after its discontinuation.

Consult an AME about a return to flight duties when methyldopa has been prescribed.

Generic name: *methylphenidate*
Brand name: *Ritalin*
Usual dose: (varies)

Methylphenidate is used to treat certain behavioral disorders that occur in older children. It is also used to treat narcolepsy in adults, a condition in which sleep occurs suddenly and uncontrollably.

In addition to its desired therapeutic effects, methylphenidate may cause adverse side effects. Examples of these side effects that are of significance to pilots include nervousness, dizziness, fever, and headache. Insomnia may also occur.

Suspend all flight activities while using methylphenidate. The strong effects of methylphenidate and the adverse effects of narcolepsy are disabling for a pilot.

Consult the FAA about possible future flight activities when methylphenidate has been prescribed.

Generic name: *nortriptyline*
Brand names: *Aventyl, Pamelor*
Usual dose: 75–100 mg per day

Nortriptyline is used to treat the symptoms of depression. Feelings of depression may vary from feeling "low" to deep despair and thoughts of suicide.

In addition to its therapeutic effects nortriptyline may show a number of side effects, which vary widely in their expression. Blood pressure may increase or decrease, the heart may beat faster, confusion or anxiety may occur, and the skin may be affected with a rash or itchiness. Nausea or abdominal cramps may also occur.

The half-life of nortriptyline is about forty hours. It requires nine days from the last dose of nortriptyline to its essential clearance from the body.

Use of nortriptyline can lessen a pilot's capability. In addition, the depressed state itself reduces flying ability. Therefore, avoid flying while taking nortriptyline.

Consult an AME or the FAA prior to resuming flight duties when nortriptyline has been prescribed.

Generic name: *oxazepam*
Brand name: *Serax*
Usual dose: (Varies)

Oxazepam is used to treat excessive feelings of anxiety. In addition to its desired therapeutic effect, oxazepam may cause adverse side effects. Examples of these side effects that are of significance to pilots include dizziness, headache, and drowsiness.

The half-life of oxazepam is about thirty-six hours. It takes seven full days from the last dose to the time of its essential clearance from the body.

Suspend flight activities while taking oxazepam. Because it is such a potent drug, flight activities cannot be maintained with safety. Excessive feelings of anxiety can themselves be disabling for a pilot as well.

Consult an AME about the resumption of flight duties when oxazepam has been prescribed.

Generic name: *penicillamine*
Brand name: *Cuprimine*
Usual dose: (varies)

Penicillamine is used in the treatment of rheumatoid arthritis and a number of other conditions. The other conditions usually involve some disability due to improper copper metabolism.

In addition to its desired therapeutic effects, penicillamine may cause unwanted side effects. Examples of these side effects that are of significance to pilots include various skin reactions, nausea and vomiting, aggravation of a stomach ulcer, and pain in the abdomen.

Suspend flight activities while taking penicillamine. It is a potent drug. Consult with an AME or the FAA when use of penicillamine begins in regard to future flight duties.

Generic name: *pentazocine*
Brand name: *Talwin*
Usual dose: (varies)

Pentazocine is used for the relief of moderate to severe pain. It is subject to drug abuse.

In addition to its desired therapeutic effects, pentazocine may cause unwanted side effects. Examples of these side effects that are of sig-

179

nificance to pilots include dizziness, headache, diarrhea, and blurring of vision.

The half-life of pentazocine is about three hours. It takes fifteen hours from the last dose to the essential clearance of the drug from the body.

Suspend all flight activities while using pentazocine. When the use of pentazocine is ended, consult with an AME about the resumption of flight activities. A consideration in the return to pilot duties following use of pentazocine is the status of the condition for which the drug was taken.

Generic name: *phenmetrazine*
Brand names: *Obeval, Preludin*
Usual dose: 50–75 mg per day

Phenmetrazine is used to reduce the appetites of persons trying to lose weight by dieting. It is subject to abuse and should not be used for more than a relatively short time.

In addition to its desired therapeutic effects, phenmetrazine may cause adverse side effects. Examples of these side effects that are of significance to pilots include rapid heart rate, restlessness, dizziness, and headache. Mental functioning may be altered, producing aberrant behavior.

Suspend all flight activities while using phenmetrazine. Its side effects can impair pilot performance. When use of phenmetrazine is ended, consult an AME about the resumption of flight activities.

Generic name: *phentermine*
Brand names: *Adipex, Ambese, Fastin, Ionakraft, Ionamin, Obecaps, Obesamead, Ona-Mast, Panshape, Phentrol, Rolaphent, Teramine, Tora, Waynamine, Westrol*
Usual dose: 30 mg per day

Phentermine is used to assist in losing weight by depressing the appetite. It is subject to abuse.

In addition to its desired appetite-suppressing effect, phentermine may cause adverse side effects. Examples of these side effects that are of special significance to pilots include dizziness, restlessness, headache, and diarrhea.

Suspend all flight activity while taking phentermine. Its effects are powerful enough to be disabling for a pilot.

Consult an AME about the resumption of flight activities when phentermine is prescribed.

Generic name: *prochlorperazine*
Brand name: *Compazine*
Usual dose: (varies)

Prochlorperazine is used to treat mental disorders, to help to relieve severe tension and anxiety, and to control nausea and vomiting.

In addition to its desired therapeutic effects, prochlorperazine may cause unwanted side effects. Examples of these side effects that are of significance to pilots include a lack of muscular coordination, headache, mental disturbance, and skin itch or rash.

The half-life of prochlorperazine is about twenty-four hours. When use of prochlorperazine is ended, it takes five days for essential clearance of the drug from the body.

Suspend all flight activities while using prochlorperazine. It is a potent drug and its use must be considered disabling for a pilot.

Consult an AME or the FAA about future pilot duties when prochlorperazine is prescribed.

Generic name: *protriptyline*
Brand name: *Vivactyl*
Usual dose: 15–40 mg per day

Protriptyline is used to help individuals overcome the feelings associated with depression. These may include persistent feelings of gloominess, guilt, and low self-esteem.

Protriptyline and other similar drugs produce a variety of side reactions. These can affect the heart and the blood vessels, the skin, the digestive system, and other parts of the body.

Some of the side reactions, completely separate from any intended therapeutic effect, can diminish a person's flying ability. Some examples are diarrhea, skin rash, blurred vision, dry mouth, lack of mental concentration, confusion, increased heart rate, and altered blood pressure. Of particular interest to a pilot are effects on vision, reduced

181

clarity of thinking, and lessened neuromuscular coordination. A pilot who is seriously depressed must not fly. Suspend flight duties when taking protriptyline.

The half-life of protriptyline is estimated to be about forty-eight hours. It takes ten days after the last dose until the drug is essentially cleared from the body.

Consult an AME or the FAA prior to resuming flight duties when protriptyline has been prescribed.

Generic name: *rauwolfia serpentina*
Brand names: *Haltina, Hywolfia, Koglucoid, Panrau, Raubar, Raudan, Raudixin, Raufola, Rauneed, Raupen, Rauserp, Rauserpia, Rausertina, Rautina, Rauval, Rauweslin, Rauwicon, Rauwiloid, Rauwoldin, Rauwolfemms, Serbio, Serfolia, Tranquillin*
Multi-ingredient drugs: Halvertina, Rauverid, Vertensen
Usual dose: 200–400 mg per day

Rauwolfia serpentina is used to bring high blood pressure down toward normal levels. It may be used with other blood-pressure-reducing drugs. In addition, rauwolfia serpentina is used to treat certain kinds of mental disturbances. It is especially useful in the treatment of high blood pressure in persons under stress.

In addition to its desired therapeutic effects, rauwolfia serpentina may cause adverse side effects. Examples of these side effects that are of special significance to pilots include drowsiness, dizziness, mental depression, and diarrhea.

The half-life of rauwolfia serpentina is about eighteen hours. It takes four days from the last dose to the drug's essential clearance from the body.

Suspend pilot activities while taking rauwolfia serpentina. The effects of the drug are disabling for a pilot.

Consult an AME or the FAA in regard to a return to flight duties when rauwolfia serpentina has been prescribed.

Generic name: *reserpine*
Brand names: *Alkarau, Alserp, Arniloid, Cen-Serp, Contiserpine, Gene-serp, Halapine, Hiserpia, Hypersil, Lemiserp, Lopres, Masoserpine, Metz-Serp, Nelserp, Primeserp, Rauloydin, Raupresoid, Raurine, Rauserpaloid, Rau-Tab, Resercen, Reserpal, Reserpatabs, Reserpoid, Respital, Respolyn, Restran, Rolserp, Sandril, Sarpel, Seramine, Serexal, Serpahab, Serpalan, Serpaline, Serpanray, Serpasil, Serpate, Serpatin, Serpicon, Sertina, Tensin, Tranquilsin, Tri-Serp, Vioserpine, Zepine*
Multi-ingredient drugs: Butacain, Butacalm, Butiserpine, Lynnbuserp, Metatensin, Naquival, Pharmacole, Resamine, Reserbutal, Respazem, Sedaserp, Ser-Ap-Es, Serpital, Trichlortensin, Vera Tina
Usual dose: (varies)

Reserpine is used to treat high blood pressure. It may be used alone or with another blood-pressure-reducing drug. Reserpine is also used in some cases of mental disturbance.

In addition to its desired therapeutic effect, reserpine may cause unwanted side effects. Examples of these that are of significance to pilots include drowsiness, nervousness, anxiety, and headache.

The half-life of reserpine is about eighteen hours. It takes four days from the last dose to the drug's essential clearance from the body.

Suspend pilot activities while using reserpine. Its potent effects are disabling for a pilot. Consult an AME or the FAA in regard to future pilot duties if reserpine has been prescribed.

Generic name: *scopolamine*
Synonym: *hyoscine*
Brand name: *Transderm-Scōp*
Usual dose: .2 mg

Scopolamine may be used to assist in eye examinations. It causes the pupil of the eye to widen. Scopolamine is also increasingly used to prevent or control motion sickness. Astronauts have found certain scopolamine preparations useful in preventing "space motion sickness."

In addition to its desired effects, scopolamine may cause unwanted side effects. Examples of these side effects that are of significance to pilots include blurring of vision, memory loss, mental confusion, and decreased mental alertness.

The half-life of scopolamine is about three hours. It takes fifteen hours from the time of the last dose to the drug's essential clearance from the body.

Suspend pilot duties and consult an AME if a condition exists requiring treatment with scopolamine.

Generic name: *tolazoline*
Brand names: *Priscoline, Tazol, Vasodil*
Usual dose: 10–50 mg four times daily

Tolazoline acts on the arterial portion of the circulatory system. Tolazoline causes blood vessels to dilate. It has a relaxing effect on the muscles of the arteries. In addition, it may stimulate the flow of acid and other juices in the stomach. This could inflame an already irritated stomach lining or induce pain with a preexisting stomach ulcer.

Some side effects from tolazoline include queasy or uneasy feelings in the stomach, vomiting, discomfort or even pain in the lower chest or abdomen, flushing, changes in blood pressure (either up or down), and outbreak of a skin rash.

Its side effects certainly reduce a pilot's capabilities. Suspend flying and consult an AME about flight duties when tolazoline has been prescribed.

It takes about twenty-four hours after it is discontinued to essentially clear the body of the drug.

Appendix I

Schedules of Controlled Drugs

Drugs coming under jurisdiction of the Controlled Substances Act are divided into five schedules. They are as follows:

Schedule I Substances

The drugs in this schedule are those that have no accepted medical use in the United States and have a high abuse potential. Some examples are heroin, marijuana, LSD, peyote, mescaline, psilocybin, tetrahydrocannabinols, ketobemidone, levomoramide, racemoramide, benzylmorphine, dihydromorphine, morphine methylsulfonate, nicocodeine, nicomorphine, and others.

Schedule II Substances

Drugs in this schedule have a high abuse potential with severe psychic or physical dependence liability. Schedule II controlled substances consist of certain narcotic, stimulant, and depressant drugs. Some examples of Schedule II narcotic controlled substances are opium, morphine, codeine, hydromorphine (Dilaudid), methadone (Dolophine), pantopon, meperidine (Demerol), cocaine, oxycodone (Percodan), anileridine (Leritine), and oxymorphone (Numorphan). Also in Schedule II are amphetamine (Benzedrine, Dexedrine), methamphetamine (Desoxyn), phenmetrazine (Preludin), methylphenidate (Ritalin), amobarbital, pentobarbital, secobarbital, methaqualone, etorphine hydrochloride, diphenoxylate, and phencyclidine.

Schedule III Substances

Having an abuse potential lower than those in Schedules I and II, drugs in Schedule III include compounds containing limited quantities of certain narcotic drugs and nonnarcotic drugs such as: derivatives of barbituric acid except those that are listed in another schedule, glutethimide (Doriden), methyprylon (Noludar), chlorhexadol, sulfondiethylmethane, sulfonmethane, nalorphine, benzphetamine, chlorphentermine, clotermine, mazindol, phendimetrazine, and paregoric. Any suppository dosage form containing amobarbital, secobarbital, or pentobarbital is in this schedule.

Schedule IV Substances

The drugs in this schedule have an abuse potential lower than those listed in Schedules I–III and include such drugs as: barbital, phenobarbital, methylphenobarbital, chloral betaine (Beta Chlor), chloral hydrate, ethchlorvynol (Placidyl), ethinamate (Valmid), meprobamate (Equanil, Miltown), paraldehyde, methohexital, fenfluramine, diethylpropion, phentermine, chlordiazepoxide (Librium), diazepam (Valium), oxazepam (Serax), clorazepate (Tranxene), flurazepam (Dalmane), clonazepam (Clonopin), prazepam (Verstran), lorazepam (Activan), mebutamate, and dextropropoxyphene (Darvon).

Schedule V Substances

These drugs consist primarily of preparations containing limited quantities of certain narcotic drugs generally for antitussive and antidiarrheal purposes. They have the lowest abuse potential of the five schedules of controlled drugs.

Appendix II

The Two Hundred Most Frequently Used Drugs

The two hundred drugs most frequently used in office-based practice, by name of drug, generic class, and number of mentions are listed below.

Rank	Name of drug[1]	Generic class	Number of mentions in thousands
	All drugs		679,593
	200 drugs most frequently used		
1	Lasix	Furosemide	9,879
2	Ampicillin	Ampicillin	9,795
3	Penicillin[f]	Penicillin	9,736
4	Inderal	Propranolol	9,625
5	Tetracycline[f]	Tetracycline	9,478
6	Aspirin[f]	Aspirin	8,800
7	Dyazide	Combination Drug	7,435
8	Lanoxin	Digoxin	7,105
9	Polio Vaccine	Polio Vaccine	6,535
10	Valium	Diazepam	6,499
11	Diphtheria Tetanus Toxoids Pertussis	Diphtheria Tetanus Toxoids Pertussis	6,067
12	Prednisone	Prednisone	5,879
13	Motrin	Ibuprofen	5,819
14	Vitamin B_{12}[f]	Vitamin B_{12}	5,813
15	Hydrochlorothiazide[f]	Hydrochlorothiazide	5,751
16	Amoxicillin	Amoxicillin	5,506
17	Dimetapp	Combination Drug	5,377
18	Erythromycin	Erythromycin	5,363
19	Insulin	Insulin	5,248
20	Aldomet	Methyldopa	5,237
21	Digoxin	Digoxin	4,801
22	Tuberculin Tine Test[f]	Tuberculin	4,488
23	Tagamet	Cimetidine	4,482

Rank	Name of drug[1]	Generic class	Number of mentions in thousands
24	Hydrodiuril	Hydrochlorothiazide	4,395
25	Keflex	Cephalexin	4,268
26	E.E.S.	Erythromycin	4,176
27	Actifed	Combination Drug	4,019
28	Isordil	Isosorbide	3,905
29	Tylenol	Acetaminophen	3,815
30	Hygroton	Chlorthalidone	3,772
31	Tylenol w/Codeine[f]	Combination Drug	3,661
32	Phenergan[f]	Promethazine	3,541
33	Clinoril	Sulindac	3,393
34	Benadryl	Diphenhydramine	3,366
35	Amoxil	Amoxicillin	3,284
36	Kenalog	Triamcinolone	3,279
37	Diabinese	Chlorpropamide	3,204
38	Indocin	Indomethacin	3,181
39	Nitroglycerin	Nitroglycerin	3,132
40	Thyroid	Thyroid	3,071
41	Darvocet-N	Combination Drug	3,043
42	Cortisporin	Combination Drug	3,009
43	Bactrim[f]	Combination Drug	2,943
44	Cleocin[f]	Clindamycin	2,908
45	Naprosyn	Naproxen	2,857
46	E-Mycin	Erythromycin	2,844
47	Dimetane[f]	Brompheniramine	2,824
48	Phenergan w/Codeine[f]	Combination Drug	2,783
49	Septra[f]	Combination Drug	2,781
50	Premarin[f]	Estrogens	2,683
51	Lopressor	Metoprolol	2,633
52	Donnatal	Combination Drug	2,520
53	Decadron[f]	Dexamethasone	2,449
54	Neosporin	Combination Drug	2,386
55	Elavil	Amitriptyline	2,363
56	Aldactazide	Combination Drug	2,257
57	Influenza Virus Vaccine	Influenza Virus Vaccine	2,225
58	Tranxene	Clorazepate	2,217
59	Dalmane	Flurazepam	2,202
60	Potassium	Potassium Replacement Solutions	2,161
61	Aldoril	Combination Drug	2,133
62	Coumadin	Warfarin	2,106
63	Synthroid	Levothyroxine	2,105
64	Diuril	Chlorothiazide	2,101
65	Antivert	Meclizine	2,093
66	Prenatal Vitamins[f]	Multivitamins Prenatal	2,082

The Two Hundred Most Frequently Used Drugs

Rank	Name of drug[1]	Generic class	Number of mentions in thousands
67	Butazolidin[f]	Phenylbutazone	2,023
68	Monistat[f]	Miconazole	1,976
69	Celestone[f]	Betamethasone	1,970
70	Slow-K	Potassium Replacement Solutions	1,951
71	Pen-Vee-K	Penicillin	1,932
72	V-Cillin[f]	Penicillin	1,928
73	Xylocaine[f]	Combination Drug	1,887
74	Dilantin	Phenytoin	1,877
75	Timoptic	Timolol	1,875
76	Vibramycin	Doxycycline	1,844
77	Phenobarbital	Phenobarbital	1,790
78	Sinequan	Doxepin	1,766
79	Minocin	Minocycline	1,760
80	Depo-Medrol	Methylprednisolone	1,742
81	Atarax	Hydroxyzine	1,737
82	Hydrocortisone	Hydrocortisone	1,732
83	Macrodantin	Nitrofurantoin	1,724
84	Ortho-Novum	Combination Drug	1,697
85	Empirin w/Codeine[f]	Combination Drug	1,687
86	Librax	Combination Drug	1,670
87	Drixoral	Combination Drug	1,656
88	Mycolog	Combination Drug	1,649
89	Nalfon	Fenoprofen	1,642
90	Bicillin[f]	Penicillin	1,629
91	Robitussin[f]	Guaifenesin	1,617
92	Lomotil	Combination Drug	1,610
93	Fluorouracil	Fluorouracil	1,609
94	Persantine	Dipyridamole	1,605
95	Mylanta	Combination Drug	1,598
96	Ceclor	Cefaclor	1,597
97	Tetanus Toxoid	Tetanus Toxoid	1,583
98	Chorionic Gonadotropin	Chorionic Gonadotropin	1,568
99	Chlor-Trimeton[f]	Chlorpheniramine	1,559
100	Novahistine[f]	Combination Drug	1,557
101	Larotid	Amoxicillin	1,539
102	Ornade	Combination Drug	1,511
103	Aristocort[f]	Triamcinolone	1,510
104	Ativan	Lorazepam	1,503
105	Materna	Multivitamins Prenatal	1,491
106	Achromycin[f]	Tetracycline	1,482
107	Sudafed[f]	Pseudoephedrine	1,482
108	Combid	Combination Drug	1,443
109	Fiorinal	Combination Drug	1,435

Rank	Name of drug[1]	Generic class	Number of mentions in thousands
110	Nitro-Bid	Nitroglycerin	1,433
111	Maalox	Combination Drug	1,400
112	Ascriptin	Aspirin	1,389
113	Lidex	Fluocinonide	1,388
114	Orinase	Tolbutamide	1,352
115	Apresoline	Hydralazine	1,351
116	Librium	Chlordiazepoxide	1,343
117	ACTH	Corticotropin	1,315
118	Gantrisin	Sulfisoxazole	1,315
119	Zyloprim	Allopurinol	1,314
120	Ser-Ap-Es[f]	Combination Drug	1,306
121	Triavil	Combination Drug	1,305
122	Esidrix	Hydrochlorothiazide	1,299
123	Ilosone	Erythromycin	1,284
124	Brethine	Terbutaline	1,273
125	Enduron	Methyclothiazide	1,253
126	Lo/Ovral	Combination Drug	1,244
127	Mellaril	Thiorizazine	1,242
128	Rondec[f]	Combination Drug	1,241
129	Norgesic	Combination Drug	1,224
130	Valisone	Betamethasone	1,222
131	Terramycin	Oxytetracycline	1,178
132	Retin-A	Tretinoin	1,178
133	Parafon Forte	Combination Drug	1,171
134	Reserpine	Reserpine	1,170
135	M-M-R	Combination Drug	1,170
136	Diphtheria Tetanus Toxoids	Diphtheria Tetanus Toxoids	1,167
137	Naldecon	Combination Drug	1,166
138	Maxitrol	Combination Drug	1,162
139	Metamucil	Psyllium	1,160
140	Robaxin	Methocarbamol	1,138
141	Minipress	Prazosin	1,128
142	Bentyl	Dicyclomine	1,116
143	Ionamin	Phentermine	1,108
144	Quinidine[f]	Quinidine	1,107
145	Percodan[f]	Combination Drug	1,105
146	Darvon[f]	Propoxyphene	1,104
147	Cortisone	Cortisone	1,100
148	Theo-Dur	Theophylline	1,075
149	Flagyl	Metronidazole	1,072
150	Diprosone	Betamethasone	1,057
151	Methotrexate	Methotrexate	1,044
152	Estrogen	Estrogens	1,043

Rank	Name of drug[1]	Generic class	Number of mentions in thousands
153	Cytoxan	Cyclophosphamide	1,030
154	Fastin	Phentermine	1,012
155	Tolectin	Tolmetin	1,007
156	Lincocin	Lincomycin	1,003
157	Triaminic[f]	Combination Drug	997
158	Neo-Synephrine[f]	Phenylephrine	987
159	Pilocarpine	Pilocarpine	979
160	Alupent	Metaproterenol	979
161	Ovral	Combination Drug	956
162	Fluress	Combination Drug	952
163	Soma[f]	Carisoprodol	947
164	Meprobamate	Meprobamate	945
165	Chloroptic[f]	Chloramphenicol	942
166	Tigan	Trimethobenzamide	937
167	Mycostatin	Nystatin	935
168	Zaroxolyn	Metolazone	932
169	Tuss-Ornade	Combination Drug	929
170	Donnagel[f]	Combination Drug	924
171	Salicylic Acid [f]	Salicylic Acid	922
172	Desquam-X [f]	Combination Drug	909
173	Nitrogen	Nitrogen	901
174	Limbitrol	Combination Drug	900
175	Cordran[f]	Flurandrenolide	896
176	Benylin Syrup	Diphenhydramine	895
177	Lotrimin	Clotrimazole	894
178	Betadine[f]	Iodine Topical Preparations	891
179	Catapres	Clonidine	890
180	Aminophylline[f]	Aminophylline	887
181	Corgard	Nadolol	885
182	Quibron[f]	Combination Drug	882
183	Demerol	Meperidine	879
184	Flexeril	Cyclobenzaprine	879
185	Iron Preparation	Iron Preparations	874
186	Sorbitrate	Isosorbide	872
187	Tolinase	Tolazamide	870
188	Benzac[f]	Combination Drug	868
189	Tofranil	Imipramine	837
190	Medrol	Methylprednisolone	834
191	Ferrous Sulfate	Iron Preparations	834
192	Erythrocin	Erythromycin	832
193	Pavabid	Papaverine	828
194	Dramamine	Dimenhydrinate	825
195	Slo-Phyllin[f]	Theophylline	822
196	Vasodilan	Isoxuprine	818

MEDICATION AND FLYING: A PILOT'S GUIDE

Rank	Name of drug[1]	Generic class	Number of mentions in thousands
197	Topicort	Desoximetasone	805
198	Compazine	Prochlorperazine	782
199	Velosef	Cephradine	781
200	Talwin[f]	Pentazocine	779

[1] Superscript[f] denotes drug family.

Source: U.S. Department of Health and Human Services, National Center for Health Statistics, NCHS Advancedata no. 78, May 12, 1982, pp. 3–6.

Bibliography

"Aerospace Medicine, Flight Surgeon's Guide." Chapter 11 of *Drugs and the Flier*. Washington, D.C.: U.S. Department of the Air Force, 1968, pp. 11-1–11-5.

Approach: The Naval Aviation Safety Review. Norfolk, Virginia: NAVSAFECEN, U.S. Department of the Navy, December 1980 and various issues.

Armstrong, Major General Harry G. *Aerospace Medicine*. Baltimore, Maryland: Williams & Wilkins, 1961.

Carter, Dr. Earl T. "Hazards of Medication and Drugs." Chapter 13 of *Manual of Civil Aviation Medicine*. Montreal, Canada: International Civil Aviation Organization, 1974, pp. II-13-1–II-13-6.

Cutting, W. C. *Guide to Drug Hazards in Aviation Medicine*. Washington, D.C.: U.S. Government Printing Office, 1962.

DeLucien, A. G. "Bud." "Flying the Morning After the Night Before." *Helicopter Safety Bulletin*. Arlington, Virginia: Flight Safety Foundation, September/October-November/December 1980.

Dhenin, Sir Geoffrey. *Aviation Medicine*. London, England: Tri-Med Books Ltd., 1978.

Dille, J. R., and Mohler, Stanley R. "Drug and Toxic Hazards in General Aviation." *Aerospace Medicine*. 40 (February 1969): 191–195.

Dully, Captain Frank E., and Frank, Lieutenant Lawrence H. "Aviator's Guide to Self-Medication." *The Mac Flyer*. November 1979, pp. 13–14.

Goodman, L. S., and Gilman, A. *The Pharmacological Basis of Therapeutics*. New York: Macmillan Publishing Co., 1975.

Guide for AME's. Washington, D.C.: DOT-FAA, Office of Aviation Medicine, 1981.

Higgins, E. Arnold, Vaughan, John A., and Funkhouser, Gordon E. *Blood Alcohol Concentrations as Affected by Combinations of Alcoholic Beverage Dosages and Altitudes*. Washington, D.C.: U.S. Department of Transportation, FAA, Office of Aviation Medicine, April 1970.

Index to FAA Office of Aviation Medicine Reports: 1961–1980. Washington, D.C.: U.S. Government Printing Office, 1981, FAA-AM-81-1.

Julien, R. M. *A Primer of Drug Action*. San Francisco: W. H. Freeman Co., 1978.

Lacefield, Delbert J., Roberts, Patricia A., and Blossom, Curtis W. "Agricultural Aviation versus Other General Aviation: Toxicological Findings in Fatal Accidents." Washington, D.C.: U.S. Department of Transportation, FAA, September 1978.

Melmon, K. L., and Morrelli, H. F. *Clinical Pharmacology*. New York: Macmillan Publishing Co., 1972.

Mohler, Stanley R. "The Dedicated Professional Pilot: No Nicotine Addict." *Human Factors Bulletin*. Washington, D.C.: Flight Safety Foundation, July/August-September/October 1979.

Mohler, Stanley R. "Mental Functions in Safe Pilot Performance." *Human Factors Bulletin*. Washington, D.C.: Flight Safety Foundation, January/February-March/April 1979.

Mohler, Stanley R. "Pilots and Alcohol: Mix With Caution." *Human Factors Bulletin*. Washington, D.C.: Flight Safety Foundation, September/October-November/December 1980.

Randel, Hugh W. *Aerospace Medicine*. Baltimore, Maryland: Williams & Wilkins, 1971.

Ryan, L. C., and Mohler, Stanley R. "Current Role of Alcohol as a Factor in Civil Aircraft Accidents." *Aviation, Space and Environmental Medicine*, 50 (March 1979): 275–279.

Siegel, P. V., and Mohler, Stanley R. "The Current Status of Drug Use in Civil Aviation Personnel." Advisory Group for Aerospace Research and Development to North Atlantic Treaty Organization, AGARD-CPP-108, August 1972.

Stern, Edward L. *Prescription Drugs and Their Side Effects*. New York: Grosset & Dunlap, 1981.

Index

To be consistent with the text, drug names are printed in a similar format here. Generic names appear in lower-case italicized letters, brand names in italicized letters with an initial capital, and multi-ingredient names in Roman type with an initial capital. Roman numerals in parentheses following a drug name indicate the category in which the author has classified the drug. Hyphenated words are alphabetized as separate words.

196

INDEX

205